Censorship

D1471022

Other books in the Current Controversies series

Censorship

Julia Bauder, Book Editor

GREENHAVEN PRESS

An imprint of Thomson Gale, a part of The Thomson Corporation

Detroit • New York • San Francisco • New Haven, Conn. • Waterville, Maine • London

THOMSON

GALE

Christine Nasso, *Publisher*
Elizabeth Des Chenes, *Managing Editor*

© 2007 Thomson Gale, a part of The Thomson Corporation.

Thomson and Star logo are trademarks and Gale and Greenhaven Press are registered trademarks used herein under license.

For more information, contact:
Greenhaven Press
27500 Drake Rd.
Farmington Hills, MI 48331-3535
Or you can visit our Internet site at http://www.gale.com

ALL RIGHTS RESERVED
No part of this work covered by the copyright hereon may be reproduced or used in any form or by any means—graphic, electronic, or mechanical, including photocopying, recording, taping, Web distribution, or information storage retrieval systems—without the written permission of the publisher.

Articles in Greenhaven Press anthologies are often edited for length to meet page requirements. In addition, original titles of these works are changed to clearly present the main thesis and to explicitly indicate the author's opinion. Every effort is made to ensure that Greenhaven Press accurately reflects the original intent of the authors. Every effort has been made to trace the owners of copyrighted material.

Cover photograph reproduced by permission of Eddie Vincent.

LIBRARY OF CONGRESS CATALOGING-IN-PUBLICATION DATA

Censorship / Julia Bauder, book editor.
   p. cm. -- (Current controversies)
  Includes bibliographical references and index.
  ISBN-13: 978-0-7377-3277-1 (hardcover)
  ISBN-10: 0-7377-3277-6 (hardcover)
  ISBN-13: 978-0-7377-3278-8 (pbk.)
  ISBN-10: 0-7377-3278-4 (pbk.)
  1. Censorship--United States. 2. Freedom of expression--United States.
I. Bauder, Julia
  Z658.U5C395 2007
  363.31--dc22
                       2006038688

Printed in the United States of America
10 9 8 7 6 5 4 3 2 1

Contents

Chapter 1: Should Offensive Speech Be Censored?

Yes: Offensive Speech Should Be Censored

Chapter 3: Should Pornographic and Violent Material Be Censored?

Yes: Pornographic and Violent Material Should Be Censored

No: Pornographic and Violent Material Should Not Be Censored

Chapter 4: Should Speech That Endangers National Security Be Censored?

Foreword

By definition, controversies are "discussions of questions in which opposing opinions clash" (Webster's Twentieth Century Dictionary Unabridged). Few would deny that controversies are a pervasive part of the human condition and exist on virtually every level of human enterprise. Controversies transpire between individuals and among groups, within nations and between nations. Controversies supply the grist necessary for progress by providing challenges and challengers to the status quo. They also create atmospheres where strife and warfare can flourish. A world without controversies would be a peaceful world; but it also would be, by and large, static and prosaic.

The Series' Purpose

The purpose of the Current Controversies series is to explore many of the social, political, and economic controversies dominating the national and international scenes today. Titles selected for inclusion in the series are highly focused and specific. For example, from the larger category of criminal justice, Current Controversies deals with specific topics such as police brutality, gun control, white collar crime, and others. The debates in Current Controversies also are presented in a useful, timeless fashion. Articles and book excerpts included in each title are selected if they contribute valuable, long-range ideas to the overall debate. And wherever possible, current information is enhanced with historical documents and other relevant materials. Thus, while individual titles are current in focus, every effort is made to ensure that they will not become quickly outdated. Books in the Current Controversies series will remain important resources for librarians, teachers, and students for many years.

In addition to keeping the titles focused and specific, great care is taken in the editorial format of each book in the series. Book introductions and chapter prefaces are offered to provide background material for readers. Chapters are organized around several key questions that are answered with diverse opinions representing all points on the political spectrum. Materials in each chapter include opinions in which authors clearly disagree as well as alternative opinions in which authors may agree on a broader issue but disagree on the possible solutions. In this way, the content of each volume in Current Controversies mirrors the mosaic of opinions encountered in society. Readers will quickly realize that there are many viable answers to these complex issues. By questioning each author's conclusions, students and casual readers can begin to develop the critical thinking skills so important to evaluating opinionated material.

Current Controversies is also ideal for controlled research. Each anthology in the series is composed of primary sources taken from a wide gamut of informational categories including periodicals, newspapers, books, U.S. and foreign government documents, and the publications of private and public organizations. Readers will find factual support for reports, debates, and research papers covering all areas of important issues. In addition, an annotated table of contents, an index, a book and periodical bibliography, and a list of organizations to contact are included in each book to expedite further research.

Perhaps more than ever before in history, people are confronted with diverse and contradictory information. During the Persian Gulf War, for example, the public was not only treated to minute-to-minute coverage of the war, it was also inundated with critiques of the coverage and countless analyses of the factors motivating U.S. involvement. Being able to sort through the plethora of opinions accompanying today's major issues, and to draw one's own conclusions, can be a complicated and frustrating struggle. It is the editors' hope that Current Controversies will help readers with this struggle.

Introduction

"Despite the First Amendment, freedom of speech has never been absolute in the United States."

"Congress shall make no law respecting an establishment of religion, or prohibiting the free exercise thereof; or abridging the freedom of speech, or of the press; or the right of the people peaceably to assemble, and to petition the Government for a redress of grievances." So reads the First Amendment to the U.S. Constitution, which its author, James Madison, called the "most valuable amendment" in the entire Bill of Rights. Yet despite the First Amendment, freedom of speech has never been absolute in the United States. Speech that has been considered to be obscene, treasonous, or otherwise harmful has frequently been restricted. In 1873 the U.S. Congress passed the Comstock law, which forbade people from sending "lewd, indecent, filthy or obscene" materials through the U.S. Post Office. Around 350 people were convicted under the law, and dozens of books that are now considered classics, including James Joyce's *Ulysses* and Voltaire's *Candide*, were banned. The Comstock law was never officially repealed, although it is no longer enforced.

Certain types of political speech have also been censored. The U.S. Congress has passed Sedition Acts during times of unrest, such as in the late 1790s and during World War I, that forbade Americans from criticizing some aspects of the government and its policies. Several prominent members of the American Socialist Party, including general secretary Charles Schenck and five-time presidential candidate Eugene Debs, were convicted under this law for speaking out against World War I. Both men appealed their convictions all the way to the Supreme Court, but in both cases the Supreme Court upheld their convictions.

The United States is not unique in giving its citizens the right to free speech, nor in declining to make that freedom of speech absolute. Many other countries also have laws that protect the free speech rights of their citizens. One-hundred-fifty-seven countries are parties to the International Covenant on Civil and Political Rights, a treaty that declares, "Everyone shall have the right to freedom of expression; this right shall include freedom to seek, receive and impart information and ideas of all kinds, regardless of frontiers, either orally, in writing or in print, in the form of art, or through any other media of his choice." However, the treaty continues to say that those free speech rights may be restricted to protect the rights of others, national security, public order, and "public health or morals." It even specifically demands that "any advocacy of national, racial or religious hatred that constitutes incitement to discrimination, hostility or violence shall be prohibited by law."

The United States has been reluctant to ban such "hate speech"; there is a general consensus that such a ban would violate the First Amendment. Many other democratic countries that generally protect free speech rights have not had such reservations. Canada, Australia, and much of western Europe have laws limiting speech that defames various racial, ethnic, and religious groups, that is antigay, or that denies that the Holocaust took place. These laws are actively enforced and have led to arrests, fines, and in some cases jail sentences.

In one such instance, British historian David Irving was sentenced to three years in prison in Austria in 2006 for denying the Holocaust. His conviction was based on a speech that he gave in that country in 1989 in which he stated that there were no gas chambers at the Auschwitz concentration camp. A bit farther south, renowned journalist Oriana Fallaci was due to be put on trial in Italy in December 2006 for her book *The Force of Reason*, which was alleged to be offensive to Islam. The book was harshly critical of that religion and of European elites who, Fallaci claimed, failed to recognize the threat that Muslim immigrants posed to Europe. (Fallaci died of cancer before her trial could be held.)

It is worth keeping in mind when reading the following viewpoints, which primarily address the situation in the United States, that similar debates over free speech have occurred around the world and that other democratic countries have often reached very different conclusions about the need for censorship. Even within the United States, many people passionately disagree over whether certain types of harassing and obscene speech ought to be protected by the First Amendment, whether children should have full First Amendment rights, and whether the freedom of the press extends to the right to publish information that could harm national security. These are the questions debated by the authors in *Current Controversies: Censorship.*

CHAPTER 1

Should Offensive Speech Be Censored?

Chapter Preface

Beginning on January 1, 2002, the Australian state of Victoria made it illegal to "engage in conduct that incites hatred against, serious contempt for, or revulsion or severe ridicule of" a person or group because of that person or group's race or religion. The law was intended to help curb so-called Islamophobia: hatred of and discrimination against Muslims.

The highest-profile lawsuit brought under the law in its first years involved Catch the Fire Ministries, a Christian group. The Islamic Council of Victoria sued two ministers with Catch the Fire, Daniel Scot and Danny Nalliah, claiming that the ministers had vilified Islam in a seminar that they had presented. Scot and Nalliah admitted that they had criticized Islam, but said that their criticisms were factual and true.

Scot used to live as a Christian in Pakistan, but he was forced to flee to Australia after he was charged with blasphemy—an offense that can carry the death penalty in Pakistan—for refusing to convert to Islam. Once in Australia, he became concerned about the number of Australians who were converting to Islam without, he felt, a full understanding of the troubling side of the religion. To help educate Australians he began giving seminars in which he explained what the Koran and other Muslim holy texts have to say about jihad (holy war), the status of women, and other sensitive topics.

The lawsuit against Scot and Nalliah put the judge who heard it in a very difficult position. Although the judge was not an expert in Islam, he was expected to rule upon complex theological arguments. In the end, he decided that Scot and Nalliah had vilified Islam and ordered them to apologize. They refused.

In response to the lawsuit many Christians began going to Islamic events, gathering evidence that Muslims had said similarly defamatory things about Christians and suing those Muslims. Some of the Muslims were also convicted of vilifying another's religion.

Do lawsuits such as these represent a positive step toward stamping out hatred and intolerance, or are they simply censorship? This is the question debated by the authors in the following chapter.

Racist Hate Speech Should Be Banned

Alexander Tsesis

Alexander Tsesis is a professor of law who has taught at Marquette University Law School, the University of Pittsburgh School of Law, and Chicago-Kent College of Law. He is the author of Destructive Messages: How Hate Speech Paves the Way for Harmful Social Movements, *from which the following viewpoint is excerpted.*

Stereotypes help actors legitimize their acts in ways that they would find unfair and inequitable if they themselves were the objects of the vitriol. Moreover, persons who degrade others based on their race or ethnic origin also diminish the general welfare of society by increasing the prevalence of prejudices that deny social goods to persons based on arbitrary characteristics. Therefore, representative democracy should protect minority civil rights by enacting narrowly tailored laws prohibiting instigatory speech that substantially increases the likelihood of discrimination. Lawmakers should be cognizant of historically persecuted groups' concerns about messages that are purposefully spread to harm them, their families, and friends. It is naive, or at least dismissive of historical realities, to believe that all propagandists who spread messages of hate and destruction, except those calling for immediate action, will be content with words.

The premises of hate speech contravene universal fair treatment; they are meant to mark certain persons as unworthy of empathy: these persons become expendable means to advancing the interests of those holding power. This process seeks to invalidate minority aspirations and preferences. Outgroups are viewed as merely instrumental for others, their goals are considered unimportant. Hate speech is intolerant and therefore could never be part of a universal rule of reciprocal action.

Stereotypes do not reflect the truth even when they emerge victorious in the marketplace of ideas, as pro-slavery thought did in the antebellum South or anti-Semitism did in postimperial Germany. Since persons join societies to protect their fundamental rights and to reap the benefits of basic rights, a better test of truth is the extent to which speech seeks, discovers, and establishes institutions conducive for human rights to thrive. Bigots use derogatory cultural stereotypes to deny outgroups the very rights they find essential and which they expect others to honor. The right to self-expression does not trump other people's dignitary rights.

Hate Speech Is Dehumanizing

Destructive messages deny the personhood of minorities. They establish paradigms of thought that are meant to solicit a group's adherents to act inhumanely. Hate speech poses a threat to social stability and individual safety. Infringements of an individual's personhood are intrinsically unjust. The value of such denigrating speech is so low that it pales in comparison to the interests in life, liberty, and self-preservation which it tries to incite others to violate. While hate speech is shrouded in the democratic mantle of freedom of expression, it seeks to undermine a designated group's sense of personal integrity and civic assurance.

To illustrate this point, suppose that some people burn a cross in their community, set up a sign informing Jews they are unwelcome, or design an Internet site committed to instigating a race war. All of these acts, explicitly or subtly, let people know that they are unwelcome, that the acts are designed to terrorize them, and that other community members plan to shun and exclude them. With the added voice of charismatic leaders, devotees of misethnicity [institutionalized hatred of certain ethnic groups] become further entrenched in cultural ideologies. Once any social problem—for example, unemployment—is ideologically linked to a particular out-group, demagogues can offer solutions whose fierceness is commensurate with how entrenched in a culture the evoked stereotypes are.

Our views of the world and perspectives of others are per-meated with presumptions and categorizations acquired from the symbols commonly used in our cultures. Language is not only a means for exposing and discerning truth, but also for stifling and misrepresenting it. Derogatory misethnic stereo-types pave the way for harmful social movements because they create a despised class of people. It is difficult to justify injustices because humans have an innate, although surmount-able, proclivity for empathy. However, when a salient group is thought to embody undesirable traits—being devoid of hu-man qualities, corrupting society, and posing a threat to women and children—its personhood can be ignored.

The most effective propaganda rejects or disregards the humanity of particular groups of people. Everyone in the out-group is classed together. They are all deemed subordinate and socially repulsive. Misethnic insults convey "the message that distinctions of race are distinctions of merit, dignity, sta-tus, and personhood." Such speech disregards or outright re-jects the humanness of its object, making it easier to commit aggressive acts with moral equanimity. It rejects the notion that each individual is intrinsically important and fit for social membership. Once the others have become mere chimeras with purely wicked attributes, they no longer have any funda-mental rights, and society, surely, is no longer obliged to pro-tect their basic rights.

To soothe their conscience for exterminating Jews with poisonous gas, Nazis first characterized them as vermin, thereby justifying their fumigation. On a different continent, slave owners shackled slaves hand and foot and sold them into slavery after they were convinced blacks were a species of man inferior to whites. The guilt associated with treating people unfairly can be eviscerated by messages whose effectiveness comes from their protracted potency to indoctrinate large numbers, and sometimes almost an entire nation, of followers. Misethnic insults are meant to establish a basis on which persecution and acts as brutal as murder can be rationalized. Supremacists recruit followers by proclaiming their moral, religious, and cultural superiority relative to weaker groups. Frontier people who forcefully stole Native American lands thought they were doing Indians a favor by "civilizing" and bringing Christianity to them. When outgroups are regarded as parasitic, their right to personal security is not deemed genuine. Without accounting for this part of the equation, the strand uniting ideology with socially acceptable misethnic violence is lost.

Hate Speech Breeds Discrimination

Hate groups use destructive messages and deprecations to build up their infrastructure while they wait for their often slow-acting poison to act on the body politic. The Nazis could not have come to power if anti-Semitism had not first become acceptable in the preceding years. They incorporated slogans into their *weltanschauung* [worldview] that had become part of popular culture (e.g., "The Jews Are Our Misfortune") and took them to their logical conclusion: genocide. Likewise, blacks had been degraded since the sixteenth century in parts of the American colonies. The long-standing commitment to slavery made it impossible to get states like South Carolina to ratify the U.S. Constitution without including provisions tolerant of that undemocratic institution. Misethnicity often takes a long time to spread its roots. It was not until the legend of the roaming Indian became popular on a national level that a notorious Indian conqueror, Andrew Jackson, could push the Indian Removal Act through Congress and justify land theft under the guise of law. Hate speech rarely results in only short-term harms. More commonly, it is developed by succeeding generations and becomes part of social interaction and political culture.

The purpose of destructive messages is to perpetuate inequalities in opposition to democratic values. Calumnies reject the validity of outgroup claims to social-compact benefits. Propagandists call on others, and express a personal commitment, to undermining government's obligation to safeguard the well-being of all citizens. Their expressions impair people's ability to realize dreams and to have their rights fully protected. The notion that propaganda is essential to the assent of tyrannical regimes is not new. In *The Republic*, Plato drew attention to the central role charismatic leaders play in a degenerating democracy. He recognized that agitators systematically generate broad support by denigrating their enemies with false accusations. Plato also had the foresight to realize that the freedoms people enjoy in a democracy can be exploited to establish mob rule and, subsequently, tyranny. Demagogues look for colloquialisms and well-established symbols to make their messages more easily understood. This endears them to the masses and drafts others to exploit minority members for ulterior motives.

A society cannot simultaneously cultivate discriminatory attitudes and be committed to protecting personal rights.

When orators, especially those with a following, begin speaking of purging society's diversity, the potential for discrimination against outgroups rises. Speakers use historical stereotypes purporting the inferiority of outgroups to incite violence. Hate crimes are not perpetrated in a psychological and social vacuum. Oratory enunciated against outgroups with the explicit intent to harm them can inflame audiences to commit violent actions. Hate speech reinforces existing prejudices and provides the false information necessary to create new ones. The intensification and development of prejudice is a social evil that threatens harmonious democracy.

The repeated expression of racist and ethnocentric invective makes commonplace the view that minorities are innately unworthy of full constitutional rights. It becomes an affront to even suggest there is anything wrong with unjustly treating people who are commonly disparaged. Persons reared on misethnic linguistic paradigms are confused, offended, and even angered by anyone who questions these injustices; after all, they are only committed against those apelike, parasitic, lazy fools whose very presence pulls down all society.

Hate Speech Harms Democracy

A society cannot simultaneously cultivate discriminatory attitudes and be committed to protecting personal rights. Human integrity is guaranteed only by states where each individual's liberty is viewed as equally precious, no matter how powerful or powerless his or her race and ethnic group may be. Persons living in any organized society with formal laws and rules owe one another a reciprocal duty of humanitarian treatment. This cannot be achieved where persons treat others in ways they would find unfair if treated so themselves, and where hate propaganda is allowed to influence the development of social institutions. The quest for justice entails using reason to arrive at empathic and tolerant customs, rules, and regulations. The libertarian argument that minority rights can best be protected by uninhibited and unrestricted hate propaganda is counterintuitive given the long-term dangers associated with hate speech. Hate messages are opposed to the spirit of social contract theory, which requires respect for the rights of the contractees. Only when everyone's liberty interests are recognized is there hope of ending the sometimes deadly blights of racism and ethnocentrism. Identification with other people's dignity derives best from a cosmopolitan conception of human consciousness and the expression of empathy toward diverse individuals.

Although hate speech does not always lead to organized supremacism, it is a necessary ingredient to that end. Permitting persons or organizations to spread ideology touting a system of discriminatory laws or enlisting vigilante group violence gradually leads to the erosion of democracy. So it was in the Weimar Republic, where the repeated anti-Semitic propaganda of vulgar ideologues like Julius Streicher, who published perverse attacks against Jews in *Der Stürmer*, chipped away at the democratic experiment in pre–World War II Germany. His weekly stories of Jewish ritual murder and rape of Christian children hit their mark: the German psyche. It is truly eerie, now, looking at photographs relating the effectiveness of Nazi propaganda: respectable-looking adults in suits and dresses listening to long lectures on Jewish inferiority; children, barely able to stand on their two feet, raising their right arm in a Nazi salute. So, too, with racism in America. Senator John Calhoun, Congressman Henry Wise, and other powerful racist orators misled the public about the supposedly benevolent slave owner, feeding his slaves and treating them like his own children. Omitted were the reputable accounts of slaves being beaten to death, having their limbs cut off for running away, getting their front teeth knocked out as a form of branding, and other tortures captured in eyewitness books such as *American Slavery As It Is: Testimony of a Thousand Witnesses*. The repeated inculcation of supremacism proved effective in misrepresenting blacks as movable property. Giants of human rights advocacy, such as Theodore Weld, Angelina and Sarah Grimké, Frederick Douglass, and William Lloyd Garrison, were unable to win the country to their abolitionist views. The contradictory, dual American messages—of the legitimacy of human bondage and civil liberty—compromised the ideals of equality.

Free Speech Is Not Absolute

Free speech is not an absolute right. It is constrained by the rights of others to enjoy their lives and liberties without fear of hate groups expostulating on their inferiority and advocating their enslavement, extinction, or disenfranchisement.

Recognizing ethnic differences is not, of course, in and of itself detrimental. In fact, celebrating diversity facilitates civil interactions. The danger arises when individuals disseminate legitimizing discourse in order to organize exclusionary movements.

The composite good of a society is reduced by the publication of material intent upon instigating pain and suffering for a particular group.

Placing no limits on speech—not even on expressions blatantly intended to make life miserable for minorities—preserves the rights of speakers at the expense of targeted groups. One person's right of expression should not infringe on other people's rights. This is a chief principle behind limits on speech via defamation statutes, zoning regulations, and obscenity laws. Everyone's right to develop personally is equally important both to individuals and to society. Successful hate speech, which gains a broad following, has the potential to inhibit the targets from full self-realization and reduces the total available talents in the social pool of abilities. Spain, for instance, hurt itself culturally and economically by expelling its Jewish population in 1492. The Expulsion came after years of Inquisition propaganda, and hurt both the exiled Jews and the remaining Spanish population. Teachings by zealous preachers like Vincent Ferrer, a later-canonized Dominican monk, in the late fourteenth and early fifteenth centuries, brought on a nationwide anti-Jewish hysteria. By ridding the country of Jews, the Spanish monarchs, Ferdinand and Isabella, were carrying out the religious doctrines of the Inquisition. The economic consequences were grave. Many commercial enterprises in Seville and Barcelona, for instance, were ruined. "Spain lost an incalculable treasure by the exodus of Jewish . . . merchants, craftsmen, scholars, physicians, and scientists," wrote the encyclopedic Will Durant, "and the nations that received them benefited economically and intellectually." Anti-Jewish preaching in Spain influenced a wide social segment of the population, and the result was devastating both for the Jews who fled and for the country that renounced them on dogmatic grounds.

The composite good of a society is reduced by the publication of material intent upon instigating pain and suffering for a particular group. Adopting an unrestrictive point of view on free speech assumes the character of dogma, taking a right as an ultimate duty and ignoring the ultimate end of constitutional government, which is the well-being of all social members. Thus, when the speech of some social contractees interferes with the right of others to live contented lives, it is speech, and not the essential rights necessary for well-being, that must be limited.

Speech is not the end of social justice. The First Amendment does not protect all expressions. It is designed to maintain an open dialogue about individual rights and overall welfare. In and of itself, speech is a neutral medium that can just as easily promote fascism as democracy, or justify genocide as civil rights. Ideological declarations that create irrational prejudices will not protect other rights. Hate messages can sway attitudes by their congruity with accepted exclusionary social schemas and linguistic paradigms. They can impress themselves on avowed supremacists and can also recruit young neophytes who, when they become adults, will carry on the tradition of vertical racial and ethnic hierarchies. Misethnic speech increases the reaches and continuity of racism and ethnocentrism in society. The hatreds underlying traditional scapegoating will not always burgeon into action. For that, social strains have to be at a peak. But they will lie dormant until the season is right for the noxious ideas to bud into violence.

Harboring hate speakers poses a threat to personal liberties. It enervates the very democratic ideals from which free speech arises. The overindulging of demagogues, therefore, deteriorates the commitment to fundamental rights that lies at the heart of people's decision to join together and reside in communities. The risks that misethnic propaganda poses to social well-being are enormous. They significantly increase the likelihood that violence will be perpetrated against minorities and that their safety will be jeopardized. Further, propaganda is subversive to social order because it infuses stress into intergroup relations.

Hate Speech Leads to Aggression

Diatribe is intended to communicate aggression and to influence behavior. Hate speakers do not proclaim their views to engage listeners in intellectual debate; rather, they try to gain adherence to their destructive ideals. Hate speech functions to justify social injustices and to champion their rectitude.

While the Constitution protects freedom of speech, 'it is not a suicide pact.'

The hate message is often meant to curtail inclusiveness and is stated in the context of a historical discourse, which supports existing power structures. It also perpetuates a mindset that views group interactions in the context of insiders with common interests and outsiders undeserving of basic human rights. The political implication of this self-perpetuating system is that it creates a racial identity that artificially classifies persons' mental abilities and moral uprightness on the basis of artificial semantic constructs. The effects of misethnicity, then, go far beyond personal attitudes, seeping into subordinating social structures that limit minority rights.

Knowing the dangerous potentials of hateful diatribe, we ought to be leery about the social-justice claims of a doctrine that extols speech above all other democratic values. Speech that furthers social welfare and justice is on a different par from invectives designed to undermine them. Preserving civility is vital to a diverse society. Hate propaganda, on the other hand, makes it easier to channel aggression and enmity, thereby creating a chimerical enemy and distracting attention from genuine problems. Many politicians, in fact, obtain and retain offices by eliciting fears about historical outgroups and their allegedly evil ways.

The potential that today's fringe groups will gain political ascendency through sustained ideological dissemination calls for legislative vigilance. A democratic state need not tolerate demagogues who manipulate constitutional provisions for spreading deadly ideology designed to enlist followers and eventually enact discriminatory laws. The state need not sit idly by while the freedoms of democracy are exploited by powerful social forces bent on undermining justice and the common good. While the Constitution protects freedom of speech, "it is not a suicide pact," [to quote Justice Robert H. Jackson from 1949].

Hate Speech Threatens Minorities' Rights

In a constitutional democracy, each person's rights must be respected as intrinsically valuable. Society and the state must honor and respect each person and protect his or her rights. A democracy is a quilt of individuals sown together by just principles and fair laws. Each person adds color and contributes to its overall pattern. When propagandists undo the threads that bind all the separate parts, the entire structure is weakened and is threatened with decay and collapse.

Destructive messages are contrary to the principles of egalitarian society because they influence people to deny the humanity of outgroups and refuse them equal treatment. Repudiating someone's personhood is in effect denying that the reciprocal duty of humanity and the imperative to empathetic treatment are at all applicable to him or her. Misethnists spread misinformation, invoking traditional images of ethnic stratification, to legitimize arbitrary laws and intolerant private conduct. The followers of racialist ideology seek to deprive minorities of basic needs, such as adequate education and unbiased law enforcement, which are essential for self-realization and personal security.

The more often insulting words about minorities are repeated, the easier it becomes to treat them uncompassionately without incurring much resistance. Hate propaganda, thus, creates not only immediate threats or harm, but also long-lasting residual effects on the entire community where it becomes incorporated into daily conversations, sermons, and political diatribe.

The ramifications of hate speech include elevated anxiety about social stability. It decreases social contentment by denying minorities the opportunity to fulfill their aspirations. Demeaning affronts to minorities are also opposed to numerous constitutional ideals: self-realization, personal security from the tyranny of the majority, an unmolested and good life, secure property rights, and equal say in picking political representatives. Bigotry elicits preconceptions that have led to countless crimes against humanity. It interferes with democratic governments' efforts to achieve harmony among a variegated population. Instead of furthering everyone's interests, hate messages denigrate groups that have been historically vulnerable to victimization. How can it be argued that calls for murder, rapine, and enslavement promote everyone's welfare? Rather than being a means to elicit more political, ethical, and social opinions, which the right to free speech is meant to facilitate, misethnic insults dismiss the opinions of minorities based on no more than mere assertions of their inferiority.

Hate Speech Stifles Debate

The argument that hate speech furthers democracy is difficult to fathom, given that its very intent is to stifle political debate on the issues and replace it with false accusations and brutal solutions. It presents no ideas of any worth in improving peoples lives, increasing people's knowledge, or furthering the human quest for social justice. Laws and regulations designed to protect democratic mainstays, like procedural and substantive justice, contain counter-majoritarian safeguards. The purveyors of hatred, on the other hand, seek to rationalize why outgroups should not have an equal share of rights in the democratic community. Representative democracies are devoted to protecting the civil rights of their populations; therefore, hate speech, which argues that identifiable outgroups should not equally participate in social institutions and privileges, is incompatible with democracy.

Speech that purposefully tries to undermine minority well-being is contrary to the reciprocal duty of humanity: it rejects the ethical duty to treat others empathically and act for the increase of overall contentment. Instead of developing inclusive institutions, hate propaganda furthers injustices by drawing on a cultural vocabulary that places minority rights below ingroup interests.

Outgroups suffer at the hands of bigots advocating supremacist doctrines. Minorities are impeded in their cultural and social development because of daily uncertainties resulting from their relative political impotence and inability to fully participate in formulating substantive policies. Their safety is compromised by the real potential for violence imbedded in the cultural attitudes that give rise to hate propaganda. Misethnic speech is more than merely offensive to particular people; it carries a historical significance of exclusion and subjugation. Its overtones, therefore, are more sweeping and harmful to the life prospects of whole groups of people than are defamations. The function that free speech plays in opening the political gates to all social contractees is also eviscerated by the constant bombardment of derogatory images which degrade minority political candidates based on irrelevant criteria and elevating persons because of their opposition to equal rights.

Hate Speech Can Lead to Fascism

Misethnic antagonism that uses propaganda to instill negative attitudes toward outgroups lies along a continuum. Gradually the messages raise popular fury to a fever pitch, adding diatribe that blames traditional scapegoats for contemporary problems. When the stage is set by this preparatory groundwork, demagogues need only wait until social pressures and economic strains increase. It then becomes semantically natural for the ingroup to assign present-day troubles to a group that is supposedly culturally and nationally inimical. All that then remains is to call on the devotees to take the logical next steps: physical violence and persecution. So it was in Germany, where the hyperinflation that swept through the country after World War I catalyzed support for National Socialists. Relying on time-tested and politically refined anti-Semitism, Nazis found it relatively easy to convince most Germans that Jews deserved collective punishment for Germany's postwar woes.

Hate speech continues to play a significant role in degrading vulnerable peoples. For instance, in Mauritania and Sudan, racist common words, phrases, and symbols, which depict blacks as intellectually and religiously subservient to Arabs, perpetuate black slavery. Misethnicity is not merely a secondary social evil, it has been at the vanguard of widespread social movements. During the nineteenth century, anti-Irish sentiments existed throughout the United States. In the early part of that century, a formidable political party, the Know-Nothing Party, developed a large following through slogans denouncing immigrants and Roman Catholics. Racism against the

Irish was then popular, as is evident from cartoons depicting them as apes and referring to them as "savages." Hate speech seeds the ground for fascist and racist institutions. It is a vital ingredient in any political movement fixated on inflicting maximum harm against outgroups.

The principle of equality does not mean that everyone should be allowed to do anything he or she wishes, including insulting outgroups and calling on people to persecute them.

Fomentation of misethnic attitudes and exhortation to commit discriminatory actions is diametrically opposed to the orderly and beneficent running of a representative democracy. Misethnicity is inimical to the hopes of persons already straining under the weight of institutionalized racism and ethnocentrism. A multicultural society like the United States is strengthened and adorned by the equal treatment of different racial, ethnic, religious, and national groups. Cultural differences nourish society with unique perspectives about the empirical world and human relationships. On the other hand, hate speech promotes intergroup animosities. It disregards the personal qualities of its victims, discounts their capabilities, and augments social discontent.

Hate Speech Endangers the Common Good

While the major danger comes from state-sponsored prejudices, private groups and individuals who spread destructive messages also pose a danger, especially when they increase their power and presence through supremacist recruitment. Democracy is not only compromised by inequitable governmental actions but also by unchecked private conduct.

As social actors in a political state, persons enjoy correlative rights in respect to other citizens. Individuals living in communities established on a social contract and cooperative laws have the same right as any other contractees to advance themselves and obtain desirable resources and political offices. Laws must impartially protect social players' right to attain their desired goals. Destructive messages embed themselves in the social psyche, making it harder for minorities to achieve equal political status. Casting aspersions on outgroups is not a legitimate form of political discourse. Disparaging persons is an affront to the targets' dignity as free, conscious individuals. Moreover, such rhetoric is often accompanied by calls to perpetuate exclusionary cultural norms.

A society need not be neutral when it comes to preferring expressions that are likely to promote freedom and justice over ones with a substantial likelihood of undermining them.

The right to spread hate propaganda freely does not outweigh the right to equal treatment. Personal autonomy is not an absolute right; rather, it is limited by the right of all social players to live secure lives and the overarching aim to attain social well-being. If personal liberty were an absolute right, persons could defame, assault, batter, or murder others at will. The principle of equality does not mean that everyone should be allowed to do anything he or she wishes, including insulting outgroups and calling on people to persecute them. Instead, that principle stands for the equal right to express one's personhood and live a good life. The common good is essential for those ends; otherwise, persons would be as unprotected against others' harmful whims as they would be in a state of nature.

Demagoguery Must Be Limited

The substantial role hate propaganda plays in elevating intergroup animosity and in sanctioning hate crimes requires that there be some limits on demagoguery. The dangers associated with destructive messages are connected to their historical contexts. Symbols representing white supremacist and Nazi ideologies are dehumanizing predicates that can—as they have in the past—promote violent acts and beliefs in the future even if they do not have this immediate effect.

Judges evaluating the potential dangers of racist declarations should be aware of a minority's history with discrimination. Without such recognition they will probably see destructive messages as nothing worse than personal defamations. It is improbable that statements against ingroup participation in political and cultural life will have any effect on their social status; however, in the case of an outgroup the situation is different.

Without constitutional and legislative checks on power, the majority can run roughshod over the minority's fundamental and basic rights.

A diverse egalitarian democracy will be improved by vigorous debate on how best to integrate the variegated groups residing there. Inclusive speech, then, will hold the preeminent position, and other forms of expression will not be so highly valued. A society need not be neutral when it comes to preferring expressions that are likely to promote freedom and justice over ones with a substantial likelihood of undermining them. Taking an absolutist approach to free speech fails to acknowledge and integrate other rights, such as autonomy and life. A stand-alone theory of speech fails to account for the diverse and pluralistic aims of representative democracy. Although limitations on speech carry some danger of being abused, so too does any other law touching upon constitutional rights. The devastating potential effects of hate speech . . . warrant the careful crafting of policies and laws drafted in the least restrictive way to protect individual rights and increase overall well-being.

Bigotry is not cathartic; it is inflammatory. The longer a group goes unopposed in communicating its aggressive hatred of minorities, the more it becomes habituated in defamatory statements and unjust acts. Social attitudes are embedded in negative images and stereotypes about outgroups; these are reinforced in popular dialogue incorporating stereotypes into puns and expletives. Once individuals perceive members of identifiable groups as legitimate targets for aggression, their personal dislikes are reinforced by negative rationalizations. When stereotypes are culturally established and personally internalized through oft-repeated fallacies about outgroup characteristics, they facilitate arbitrary discrimination. Hate propaganda embellishes negative social mores and habits. It also passes malignant stereotypes, misethnic semantics, and other expressive devices, such as juxtapositions, on to children.

Placing hate speech on the level of political discourse, as Justice [Antonin] Scalia did in *R.A.V. v. St. Paul* [a 1991 Supreme Court case that overturned the city of St. Paul's ban on cross burning] legitimizes hate group participation in the political process. This decision is full of potentially dangerous consequences. Who could have accurately predicted that the Weimar Republic—which at one point even had a Jewish foreign minister, Walther Rathenau—would one day be ruled by the vociferous Nazis? The Republic fell to anti-Semitic forces who distributed their ideas throughout Germany's major institutions, including schools, the military, judiciary, and political associations. Scalia failed to reflect on any similar historical evidence about the danger hate speech poses to democracy.

Hate speech is elicited to agitate intolerance and guide adherents to fulfill violent solutions. Systematic murder, genocide, and enslavement are justified through aspersive discourse about the alleged dangers outgroups pose to society. Orators tell and retell the myth of inferiority using the framework of accepted and popularized discourse, thus desensitizing common people to the plight of victimized minorities and justifying unequal treatment of them.

Democratic Governments Must Outlaw Hate Speech

Without constitutional and legislative checks on power, the majority can run roughshod over the minority's fundamental and basic rights. An unregulated system of speech, in which more powerful forces have greater access and control over informational distribution systems, might produce what Justice [Oliver Wendell] Holmes called a "proletarian dictatorship." But it is an abuse of representative democracy to manipulate its institutions to destroy the foundations on which it is established.

Hate groups pose a threat, though not always an immediate one, to representative democracy. They use slogans that have been successfully employed to recruit and incite crowds against outgroups. Through repeated exposure to bigotry, the populace is likely to become so desensitized that it will accept oppression as a matter of course, as has happened in the past.

Violent hate speech not only advocates antidemocratic ideals, it is an intrinsic part of an overall scheme to weaken democratic institutions by attacking pluralism and inciting injustices. Unrestricted transmission of these messages threatens to undermine the political influence of diverse groups whose participation is critical to the popular-input aspect of the democratic process. The very purpose of bigotry is to exclude weaker groups from political debate. Aspersions are intended to reduce participation in governmental discourse, and destructive messages are meant to intimidate and injure. Racial hierarchies, working to the disadvantage and detriment of the less powerful, are maintained, reinforced, and revivified by a state that legitimates the use of racist and ethnocentric dialogue, especially when that dialogue makes no secret about its ultimate goal to victimize outgroups.

Representative governments are obligated to prevent incitement against a whole group of people. The legislature should act before hate propaganda endears itself into the popular culture. Tolerance and egalitarianism should not be sacrificed at the altar of an absolutist free speech doctrine. Herd mentality is best avoided by strong laws, making clear society's disapprobation of inequality and injustice. Legislation can help assure that minorities will not be tyrannized and exploited by powerful interests. Hate speech statutes will display social disapprobation for hate speech and distinguish it from legitimate forms of political dialogue. Hate speech does not further political discourse; instead, it escalates the threat to law and order.

Protests at Funerals Should Be Banned

The Columbus Dispatch

The Columbus Dispatch *is a newspaper in Columbus, Ohio. This viewpoint was written by the paper's editorial staff.*

May 30 [2006]—A recently passed Ohio House bill restricting protests at military funerals is a measured response to boundlessly offensive behavior.

House Bill 484 doesn't ban speech, rude or otherwise, but it sets up reasonable boundaries for groups that haven't been reasonable on their own. It won't prevent the vile Rev. Fred Phelps and his small "church," made up mostly of relatives, from shouting the message of hateful nonsense they've been bringing to military funerals across the country: that American troops' deaths in Iraq are God's punishment for the nation's tolerance of homosexuality. It would require, however, that Phelps and any other potential protesters stay at least 300 feet away from funeral processions, end their protests an hour before a funeral begins and not resume until an hour after the service ends. Those limitations are acceptable for any group that wants to deliver a message in a setting as somber as a funeral. They are similar to restrictions placed on protesters in many other settings, such as at political conventions and presidential speeches. Limiting the time and place of protests doesn't violate the First Amendment's guarantee of free speech. Often, such limitations are necessary to ensure public safety. The behavior of Phelps' followers outrages Americans of all stripes. This group earlier picketed at funerals of AIDS victims but switched to those of fallen troops, probably to attract more attention. Not waiting for passage of any of the protest-restriction laws pending in dozens of states, groups of patriotic motorcycle riders have taken to shadowing Phelps and his followers, inserting themselves between the "God hates fags" sign-wavers and the mourners, so the latter won't have to look at the former. Sometimes, the bikers gun their engines to drown out hateful chants. That's endearing in an only-in-America way, but having protesters drowned out by bikers still is a transgression against the privacy to which grieving families are entitled. It also could be dangerous. In the emotionally charged atmosphere of a funeral, rhetoric such as the Phelps family's could spark violence. Providing a buffer zone around a uniquely emotional event, which House Bill 484 does, preserves both the right to protest and public safety. Fortunately, the irrationally hateful inclination to torment bereaved families with insults is rare. But, for as long as Phelps' Westboro Baptist Church is taking its act on the road, and in case any future group decides on similar tactics, House Bill 484 is a reasonable antidote.

Banning the Desecration of the American Flag Would Not Be Censorship

Steven Lubet

Steven Lubet is a professor of law at Northwestern University in Evanston, Illinois.

This is a story about one liberal's newly discovered appreciation for the proposed Flag Protection Amendment. But first, a little history:

During the 1984 Republican National Convention in Dallas, a protester named Gregory Lee Johnson doused an American flag with kerosene and set it on fire, while a surrounding crowd chanted "America the red, white, and blue, we spit on you." He was arrested and charged under a Texas statute that prohibited "desecration of a venerated object." Convicted at trial and sentenced to a year in prison, Johnson appealed, setting into motion a rather surprising series of events. First, the Texas Court of Criminal Appeals—not exactly a haven of bleeding hearts, even in the pre-Bush era—reversed the conviction, noting that "the right to differ is the centerpiece of our First Amendment freedoms." But then Texas's petition for certiorari [request that the U.S. Supreme Court hear its appeal] was granted leading to speculation that the U.S. Supreme Court would reinstate the guilty verdict and uphold the flag desecration law.

In surprise number two, however, the Supreme Court's ruling in *Texas v. Johnson* held that flag burning is indeed expressive conduct, protected by the First Amendment. The greatest surprise of all, of course, was that Justices Antonin Scalia and Anthony Kennedy joined in Justice William

Brennan's majority opinion (though Kennedy also wrote a separate concurrence, expressing his unhappiness at having to reach that result, compelled as it was by the "fundamental meaning" of the U.S. Constitution). Chief Justice William Rehnquist dissented, joined by Justices Byron White, Sandra Day O'Connor, and John Paul Stevens (yet another small surprise).

Congress reacted swiftly, overwhelmingly passing the Flag Protection Act of 1989 (a preexisting federal flag-burning statute had been uncomfortably similar to the unconstitutional Texas law), which made it a crime to deface, physically defile, burn, or trample the American flag, other than for the purpose of disposal. By making it flatly illegal to burn a flag, regardless of expressive intent, it was thought that the Flag Protection Act could survive a constitutional challenge. It did not. By the same 5-to-4 margin, and in the same alignment, the Supreme Court in *United States v. Eichman* held that the statute was invalid under the First Amendment because it "suppresses expression out of concern for its likely communicative impact."

The flag [protection] amendment would not limit freedom of speech very much at all. No words or beliefs would be prohibited, no opinions would be suppressed.

Recognizing that no flag-burning statute could ever meet the constitutional test articulated in *Johnson* and *Eichman*, various groups began promoting a Flag Protection Amendment to the Constitution, providing that, "The Congress shall have power to prohibit the physical desecration of the flag of the United States." The amendment has passed the House of Representatives [several] times, . . . but it has never quite managed to obtain the two-thirds vote in the Senate necessary to send the amendment to the states for ratification. . . .

Conservatives are almost uniformly in favor of the Flag Protection Amendment, arguing that it is necessary to preserve a great symbol of national unity. Liberals tend to be opposed, fearing that no good can come of any effort to limit freedom of expression. As a lifelong liberal, my initial view was that it was a big mistake to modify the First Amendment, which has served us so well for more than 200 years. But now, surprising even myself, I have come around to the position that the proposed Flag Protection Amendment might not be quite so bad after all.

Arguments for the Flag Protection Amendment

First, national opinion polls consistently show that nearly 80 percent of Americans would vote in favor of such an amendment. Of course, widespread public support does not justify the elimination of essential personal freedoms. Protest, especially by minority groups, is often unpopular. That's why we have the Bill of Rights. On the other hand, public sentiment is an important value that liberals all too often seem to overlook. At the very least, the overwhelming approval of the flag amendment should cause us to ask just how much damage it would really do to civil liberties.

And it turns out that the flag amendment would not limit freedom of speech very much at all. No words or beliefs would be prohibited, no opinions would be suppressed. A single manner of protest would be enjoined, but the ideas behind the protest could still be expressed in a multitude of ways. As a liberal, I am in favor of broad forums for free speech, but I can still recognize a fairly negligible restriction when I see one. Had the original First Amendment included a flag exception—"Congress shall make no law abridging the freedom of speech, except for flag burning"—there is little doubt that the subsequent history of popular democracy would have been entirely unaffected. A few more protesters might have gone to jail by choice, a few more flags probably would have been burned out of frustration, and the tradition of dissent would have been otherwise unchanged.

The classic "slippery slope" argument, a staple of liberal analysis, posits that small restrictions may lead to bigger ones. But in this case, that is not true. It is tremendously difficult to amend the Constitution—requiring a two-thirds vote in each house of Congress and ratification by three-quarters of the states—so it is extremely unlikely that the flag amendment will be quickly followed by others. About 11,000 amendments have been proposed since the adoption of the Bill of Rights, yet only 17 have been adopted. Constitutional amendments are not dominoes. The Flag Protection Amendment is not the first step on a long march toward thought control.

Finally, consider a concept that we might call the "integrity of protest." The Supreme Court's legalization of flag burning may have legitimated flag abuse as a First Amendment right, but it also deprived the gesture of much of its expressive punch, making it now more of a tantrum than a demonstration of deep conviction. It means very little to say, "I can burn a flag and you can't stop me, nyah, nyah, nyah," as compared with "I am so committed to the righteousness of my cause that I am willing to risk the penalties for flag burning."

When thousands of antiwar protesters burned their draft cards in the 1960s, they faced the very real threat of prosecution and imprisonment for as long as five years. It was that fact, not merely the ignition of a small piece of paper, that helped convince the nation of the seriousness of the movement. The draft-card burnings added fuel to the antiwar campaign precisely because they were really illegal. Actions can be more persuasive when they are taken at personal cost. That is the power of true civil disobedience. At some point, we liberals might want to worry less about enabling every single expressive outburst, and more about the vitality and content of purposeful dissent.

I haven't completely lost my liberal bearings. No matter how much conservative activists fulminate, I remain quite aware that the republic is hardly endangered by flag burning, legal or otherwise. The ideals that make up America can easily survive the most vitriolic forms of protest. Therefore, I am not enthusiastic about the flag amendment and, all things considered, I think the nation would probably be just as well off without it.

The Importance of Symbols

But a powerful argument exists for the importance of a unifying national symbol—just recall the spontaneous flag displays around the country in the wake of the 9/11 terror attack. People take great comfort in our flag, and that devotion ought to be respected—especially by liberals, who are often unfairly accused of disrespect, and worse. So, in a time of increasing challenges to real civil liberties, this is one battle that need not be engaged. It would make far more sense to spend our limited political capital on amending the Patriot Act or filibustering right-wing judges, rather than on facilitating flag burning.

Liberals could show great good faith, while dispelling some shabby right-wing myths, by acknowledging that the Flag Protection Amendment will do no harm.

Racially and Sexually Offensive Speech Should Not Be Banned in the Workplace

David E. Bernstein

David E. Bernstein is a professor at George Mason University School of Law and the author of You Can't Say That! The Growing Threat to Civil Liberties from Antidiscrimination Laws, *from which the following viewpoint is excerpted.*

Jerold Mackenzie worked at Miller Brewing Company for 19 years, eventually achieving executive status and a $95,000 salary. One day, he made the career-ending mistake of recounting the previous night's episode of the sitcom *Seinfeld* to his coworker Patricia Best. In the episode, Jerry Seinfeld cannot remember the name of the woman he is dating, but he does recall that she said kids teased her as a child because her name rhymes with a part of the female anatomy. Jerry and his friend George brainstorm, but the best guesses they can come up with are the unlikely "Mulva" and "Gipple." Jerry's girlfriend breaks up with him when she realizes he doesn't know her name. As she leaves him forever, Jerry finally remembers the elusive rhyming name and calls after her, "Delores!"

Mackenzie related the details of this episode to Best, but she told Mackenzie she did not get the joke. To clarify the somewhat off-color punch line, Mackenzie gave her a copy of a dictionary page on which the word clitoris was highlighted. Best—who was apparently known to use salty language at work herself—complained to Miller Brewing officials of sexual harassment, and Miller Brewing fired Mackenzie for "unacceptable managerial performance." Mackenzie responded with a lawsuit alleging wrongful termination and other wrongs. At trial, Miller Brewing officials acknowledged that the direct cause of Mackenzie's termination was the *Seinfeld* incident and the ensuing fear of a sexual harassment lawsuit. The jury awarded Mackenzie $26.6 million, including $1.5 million in punitive damages against Best for interfering with Mackenzie's employment relationship with Miller Brewing. The verdict was later overturned on appeal because Wisconsin law does not have a law banning wrongful termination.

Miller Brewing's firing of Mackenzie may seem like an absurd overreaction, but it was very much consistent with the counsel of employment law experts. They advise employers to enforce a zero tolerance policy for any type of sex-related remarks by employees, especially those made by supervisors or executives like Mackenzie. Consultant Beau Crivello suggests, "A rule of thumb is that if you can't say it or do it in a house of worship or in front of children, then don't say it or do it at work." The rather startling message from the experts is that speech generally protected from government sanction loses that protection the moment it enters the workplace. Frank Carillo, president of Executive Communications Group, warns that just because you hear something in the media "doesn't mean you can say it [at work]. The media has a certain license to say things that the average person can't." Consultant Monica Ballard concurs: "People think that if they hear something on TV or the radio, they can say it at work. But that, of course, is not the case." Jerold Mackenzie, among others, would agree.

"Hostile Environment" Law

The roots of all of this censorship lie in the "hostile environment" component of antidiscrimination law. Beginning in the late 1970s, feminist legal scholars argued that the ban on employment discrimination against women should include a ban on sexual harassment. Sexual harassment, they argued, includes the act of subjecting women to a "hostile work environment" by exposing them to offensive speech. The speech need not be directed at any individual woman to constitute harassment. For it to qualify as harassment of a woman coworker, it is enough that the speech could reasonably be construed as hostile to women generally. Further, the determination of whether a hostile environment existed does not depend on whether anyone *intended* to make any or all of their female coworkers feel unwelcome. An innocently offered comment can as easily be charged with creating a hostile environment as a deliberate slur or threat.

The feminists achieved a great victory when the Supreme Court held in 1986 that an illegal hostile work environment exists when "the workplace is permeated with discriminatory intimidation, ridicule, and insult, . . . that is sufficiently severe or pervasive to alter the conditions of the victim's employment." Thousands of lawsuits of varying degrees of legal merit followed. Legal filings grew exponentially after the attention given to the issue of sexual harassment during the Clarence Thomas–Anita Hill hearings. Government agencies quickly produced pamphlets that urged victims of sexual harassment to file complaints and that often defined "hostile environment" far more broadly than the law justified.

Many employers responded to the growth of hostile environment law by attempting to regulate the potentially offensive speech of their employees. The result was an implicit, but nonetheless chilling, nationwide workplace speech code that banned any speech that could offend women. The Supreme Court, perhaps realizing that it had opened a veritable Pandora's box of litigation, has recently emphasized that sporadic abusive language, gender-related jokes, and occasional teasing are not enough to meet the legal test for a hostile environment. Prudent employers still feel compelled, however, to enforce speech guidelines that go well beyond what the letter of Supreme Court precedent requires.

Risks for Employers

There are several reasons for this caution. First, as four Supreme Court justices have noted in a related context, the fuzzy guidance provided by hostile environment precedents simply does not give employers a clear indication of what they must do to remain within the confines of the law. For example, while a single offensive joke will not create liability, some courts have held that a pattern of jokes by different employees can create a hostile environment. The safest route for employers is to ban *any* banter with sexual connotations, lest the aggregation of speech by different employees constitute a hostile environment. Better to be safe (if silent) than sorry.

Second, and relatedly, the severe and pervasive liability standard is sufficiently vague, good counsel sufficiently expensive, and trial judges and juries sufficiently unpredictable that employers feel compelled to settle even highly dubious claims, to avoid the risks and costs of litigation. After all, juries have awarded tens of thousands of dollars to plaintiffs in cases appellate courts later dismissed. Although clearly meritless claims rarely survive federal appellate review, no sensible attorney would advise his clients to depend on appellate courts—which can only overturn "clearly erroneous" jury verdicts—to save them from unjustified claims. This is especially true because fighting a claim to the appellate level can cost hundreds of thousands of dollars, with the costs disproportionately borne by the defendant. Victory may be sweet, but saving one's company six-digit sums by avoiding litigation entirely is even sweeter. Risk-averse employers will settle pending cases and prevent future lawsuits by cracking down on potentially offensive speech.

Third, disgruntled employees or former employees can impose large costs on employers without going to the effort and expense of filing a lawsuit, simply by complaining of harassment to the Equal Employment Opportunity Commission [EEOC]. The EEOC is legally required to investigate every complaint of sex discrimination, no matter how weak or unconvincing a complaint seems. Even a trivial complaint can lead to a broad investigation of the underlying claim, costing the employer thousands of dollars in legal fees and lost time. And petty complaints are actually encouraged by official government pronouncements that propagate inaccurate, overbroad definitions of what constitutes illegal sexual harassment. For example, an official U.S. Department of Labor pamphlet states that harassment includes cases in which a coworker "made sexual jokes or said sexual things that you didn't like, so long as the jokes made it hard to work." A very sensitive or very religious person may find that *any* sex-oriented remarks make it hard to work. Such a person is encouraged by government publications to complain of sexual harassment the first time a coworker tells a dirty joke. The offended worker will likely lose, but not before her employer wastes resources on its defense.

Even highly questionable [harassment] claims can result in large verdicts, giving employers strong incentives to heavily regulate workplace speech as a preventive measure.

Fourth, many states and localities have their own antidiscrimination laws with standards for hostile environment liability that are sometimes significantly broader than the federal laws' requirement of severe and pervasive harassment. For example, a New Jersey court held that under state law employees who forwarded one list of crude jokes to their colleagues via e-mail had created an illegal "offensive work environment," even though this act would be unlikely to create liability under federal law. Even if state and local law are no broader than federal law, employers are often at a special disadvantage when a hostile environment complaint is filed under state or local law because, unlike in the federal system, in states, administrative tribunals often make the initial ruling on hostile environment claims. Because these administrative bodies are part of executive branch agencies charged specifically with enforcing the relevant antidiscrimination laws, they naturally tend to be more sympathetic to discrimination claims and less sensitive to free speech concerns than are federal courts, which have broader responsibilities and are part of the judicial branch of government.

Racial and Religious "Harassment"

Hostile environment law has spread well beyond the sex discrimination context, with claims successfully prosecuted for race, religion, and national origin harassment. One court, for example, found that publishing religious articles in a company newsletter and printing Christian-themed verses on company paychecks constituted "harassment" of a Jewish employee. Another court found that an employee who hung in her cubicle pictures of the Ayatollah Khomeini and of Iranian protestors burning an American flag was guilty of national origin harassment against an Iranian-American employee who happened to see the display. Court rulings and EEOC guidelines suggest that religious harassment includes both a religious employee proselytizing a coworker and a secular employee ridiculing a religious coworker for the latter's beliefs.

As in the sex discrimination context, a hostile environment claim for race discrimination and other types of workplace discrimination can arise even when the speech in question was not directed at the plaintiff. For example, the EEOC charged a company with national origin harassment after a Japanese-American employee filed a complaint about the firm's advertising campaign. Some of the company's ads featured images of samurai, kabuki, and sumo wrestling to represent the firm's Japanese competitors. The employee also charged that officials of the company called Japanese competitors "Japs" and "slant-eyes." The case was eventually settled for an undisclosed amount.

Standards for racial and ethnic harassment are at least as vague as they are in the sexual harassment context, which leads to unpredictable jury verdicts. Even highly questionable claims can result in large verdicts, giving employers strong incentives to heavily regulate workplace speech as a preventive measure.

The Case of Allen Fruge

One especially meritless claim that led to a six-figure verdict involved Allen Fruge, a white Department of Energy [DOE] employee based in Texas. Fruge unwittingly spawned a harassment suit when he followed up a southeast Texas training session with a bit of self-deprecating humor. He sent several of his colleagues who had attended the session with him gag certificates anointing each of them as an honorary "Coon Ass" usually spelled "coonass"—a mildly derogatory slang term for a Cajun. The certificate stated that "[y]ou are to sing, dance, and tell jokes and eat boudin, cracklins, gumbo, crawfish etouffee and just about anything else." The joke stemmed from the fact that southeast Texas, the training session location, has a large Cajun population, including Fruge himself.

An African American recipient of the certificate, Sherry Reid, chief of the Nuclear and Fossil Branch of the DOE in Washington, D.C., apparently missed the joke and complained to her supervisors that Fruge had called her a "coon." Fruge sent Reid a formal (and humble) letter of apology for the inadvertent offense, and explained what "Coon Ass" actually meant. Reid nevertheless remained convinced that "Coon Ass" was a racial pejorative, and demanded that Fruge be fired. DOE supervisors declined to fire Fruge, but they did send him to "diversity training." They also reminded Reid that the certificate had been meant as a joke, that Fruge had meant no offense, that "Coon Ass" was slang for Cajun, and that Fruge sent the certificates to people of various races and ethnicities, so he clearly was not targeting African Americans. Reid nevertheless sued the DOE, claiming that she had been subjected to a racial epithet that had created a hostile environment, a situation made worse by the DOE's failure to fire Fruge.

Reid's case was seemingly frivolous. The linguistics expert her attorney hired was unable to present evidence that "Coon Ass" meant anything but "Cajun," or that the phrase had racist origins, and Reid presented no evidence that Fruge had any discriminatory intent when he sent the certificate to her. Moreover, even if "Coon Ass" had been a racial epithet, a single instance of being given a joke certificate, even one containing a racial epithet, by a nonsupervisory colleague who works 1,200 miles away does not seem to remotely satisfy the legal requirement that harassment must be "severe and pervasive" for it to create hostile environment liability. Nevertheless, a federal district court allowed the case to go to trial, and the jury awarded Reid $120,000, plus another $100,000 in attorneys' fees. The DOE settled the case before its appeal could be heard for a sum very close to the jury award.

The Case of Bryan Griggs

Even if a disgruntled worker decides not to take a case all the way to a jury, he can still impose costs on his boss or ex-boss by alleging that he was subjected to a hostile environment, even if he has scant supporting evidence. For example, a gay man named John Dill put his former employer, CPA Referral, in a pickle when he filed a complaint of employment discrimination with the Seattle Human Rights Department [SHRD]. Dill claimed that his ex-boss Bryan Griggs had created a "hostile work environment" for homosexuals in violation of a local antidiscrimination ordinance. According to Dill, Griggs's offensive behavior consisted of playing conservative and Christian radio shows that Dill felt conveyed an antigay message, posting a letter from a congresswoman in which she endorsed the military's policy of excluding gays, and having a note on his desk reminding himself to lobby against allowing gays to adopt children. Dill acknowledged that Griggs did not know he was gay, and Dill never told Griggs that any of Griggs's actions offended or upset him.

Dill had been employed by CPA Referral the previous fall, but Griggs had laid him off when business slowed. Griggs had allowed Dill to come back to work as a volunteer, promising him the first available paid job. Much to Griggs's surprise, Dill suddenly tendered his resignation in a letter stating that "I feel I must 'come out' and stop playing 'don't ask, don't tell.'" In his letter, Dill explained that he was leaving CPA Referral for "a supportive environment." He then filed his complaint, and the SHRD launched a full investigation of CPA Referral.

A few private employers . . . have unsuccessfully tried to claim First Amendment immunity from speech-based hostile environment claims.

The befuddled Griggs told the SHRD that he listened to the conservative talk shows to make sure they played the advertising he had paid for, and that he posted many letters from politicians to encourage political participation among his employees. Another gay employee signed an affidavit swearing that he had never perceived any antigay animus in the workplace. There seems to have been no evidence that Dill suffered antigay discrimination, and a cynic might surmise that Dill filed the complaint mainly to get revenge on Griggs for having fired him. Dill eventually withdrew his complaint, but only after Griggs had spent thousands of dollars on legal fees defending himself and his company. If Dill's goal was to punish Griggs, he managed to achieve it even without being formally vindicated by a court.

The First Amendment and Harassment

Most hostile environment employment cases have focused on whether the behavior at issue crossed the line from merely annoying or offensive conduct into conduct sufficiently severe and pervasive to meet the law's definition of creating a hostile environment. A few private employers, however, have unsuccessfully tried to claim First Amendment immunity from speech-based hostile environment claims.

There is no doubt that the Constitution protects [employees'] speech from government regulation, even when the speech conflicts with a broader regulatory scheme like hostile environment law.

The first reported hostile environment lawsuit in which the defendant invoked a free speech defense involved Lois Robinson, a welder at a Florida shipyard, who brought a case in federal court alleging that her employer, Jacksonville Shipyards, countenanced a hostile environment by permitting photos of nude and partially nude women to be displayed in various areas of her workplace. She also complained about sexual and derogatory remarks made in her presence about her and other women, and about indecent and obscene graffiti directed at her. Jacksonville Shipyards responded that the First Amendment protected at least some of this speech and asked the court to prohibit Robinson from relying on constitutionally protected speech to support her hostile environment claim.

The court ruled that the First Amendment does not protect workplace speech from employment discrimination law. The court then issued an incredibly broad injunction that banned from the Jacksonville Shipyards' workplace not only pornography but also any "sexually suggestive" material. Employees on lunch break could no longer read *Cosmopolitan* magazine or Danielle Steel novels, or listen to Eminem or Britney Spears on a Walkman.

Faulty Reasoning

The court found that the First Amendment did not protect the workplace speech at issue for several reasons, none of which is persuasive. First, the court asserted that the company was not expressing itself through the offensive expression of its employees. What the court failed to discern was that because the company was being held liable for the speech of its employees, the relevant question was whether the *employees'* speech was constitutionally protected. There is no doubt that the Constitution protects such speech from government regulation, even when the speech conflicts with a broader regulatory scheme like hostile environment law. The court failed to recognize that employers may assert a First Amendment defense on behalf of their employees, and may have their own First Amendment right to refuse to prohibit workplace speech.

Next, the court opined that the nude pinups and expressions of hostility toward women in the shipyard were not protected speech, but were discriminatory conduct in the form of creation of a hostile work environment. Here, the court was correct insofar as it pointed out that speech can sometimes be considered conduct—for example, threats, intimidation, libel, and other forms of misconduct engaged in through speech do not receive First Amendment protection. Similarly, quid pro quo harassment (e.g., "Sleep with me or else!") is not protected by the First Amendment. Arguably, the government may even regulate as an action harassing speech targeted at a particular person for discriminatory reasons. But merely labeling speech "discrimination," as the *Robinson* court did, does not make it so. Posting a nonobscene pinup or expressing a politically incorrect opinion is protected outside of the workplace, and a mere change in venue from the sidewalk to the office cannot convert such protected speech into unprotected discriminatory action. Given that most adults spend much of their time in the workplace and that almost any speech beyond the most banal is likely to offend *someone*, allowing the government to regulate any offensive speech that occurs in the workplace would invite an incredibly broad assault on freedom of speech.

Other Faulty Arguments for Speech Restrictions

The *Robinson* court next determined that regulation of offensive workplace speech was a permissible regulation of the time, place, and manner of speech. Government can regulate these aspects of speech, restricting parades and protests to certain times of the day or limiting the volume of a megaphone in a residential area. But time, place, and manner restrictions can only be valid if they do not regulate speech on the basis of the speaker's viewpoint. Thus, a rule disallowing the use of megaphones during protests in residential neighborhoods may be valid, but a rule forbidding megaphones only when they are used to criticize affirmative action would be illicit viewpoint discrimination. Hostile environment law clearly discriminates based on viewpoint. For example, hostile environment law potentially penalizes expression of the viewpoint that "women are stupid and incapable of being physicists," but not that "women are brilliant and make excellent physicists." Therefore, hostile environment law cannot be considered an appropriate time, place, and manner regulation.

If courts accepted [the] view that the First Amendment does not protect offensive speech that is very difficult or costly to avoid, much of modern First Amendment law would need to be discarded.

Finally, the court insisted that plaintiff Robinson was a "captive audience" in the shipyard and therefore the First Amendment did not protect speech that offended her. Yet we are all at times captive to expression we find offensive, in the sense that we must take action to avoid seeing or hearing it.

Nevertheless, that speech is still constitutionally protected. Of course, avoiding some types of offensive speech is relatively easy, while avoiding offensive workplace speech by finding new employment can be difficult and costly. But if courts accepted *Robinson*'s view that the First Amendment does not protect offensive speech that is very difficult or costly to avoid, much of modern First Amendment law would need to be discarded. For example, contrary to Supreme Court precedent, strikers would not have the right to picket outside their workplace, and antiabortion protestors would not have the right to assemble outside abortion clinics. The Supreme Court has even protected the right of an individual to wear a jacket displaying the phrase "F--- the Draft" inside a courthouse where many people who will see the profanity are truly a captive audience, in that they are legally required to be there. If offensive speech is thus protected when avoiding it would require committing a crime by refusing to show up in court when required, surely it must also be protected when avoiding it would only involve switching jobs. Even if the captive audience rationale *could* be used to justify speech restrictions in the workplace, any such restrictions would have to be viewpoint-neutral, which, as noted previously, hostile environment law is not.

Despite the seemingly fatal weaknesses in *Robinson*'s First Amendment analysis, many other courts have relied on it in rejecting First Amendment defenses in hostile environment cases. Most commonly in cases favorably citing *Robinson*, the plaintiff had been subjected to a pattern of severe individualized harassment, and the First Amendment defense applied only to a fraction of the behavior that allegedly created a hostile environment. However, nothing in *Robinson* limits its application to cases in which constitutionally protected expression is only a minor element. One court, in fact, cited *Robinson* favorably in a case in which the plaintiff's sole allegation was that her opponents for a union position had circulated a satirical flyer during an election campaign. The satire featured a picture of the plaintiff's head superimposed over an anonymous woman's naked body. This was tasteless, to be sure, but it was also political speech clearly protected by the First Amendment, as indicated by a landmark Supreme Court opinion protecting an even more offensive satire of Jerry Falwell that appeared in *Hustler* magazine.

Restraints on Racist Speech

Just as the injunction granted in *Robinson* created an unprecedented prior restraint (proactively censoring speech before it is spoken) on sexist speech, the California Supreme Court upheld an unprecedented prior restraint on racist speech. A jury had found that an Avis Rent A Car outlet had engaged in employment discrimination, in part by allowing an employee to repeatedly utter racial epithets targeted at the Latino plaintiffs. Besides awarding damages, the trial court issued an injunction prohibiting Avis employees "from using any derogatory racial or ethnic epithets directed at, or descriptive of, Hispanic/Latino employees of [Avis]." An appellate court limited the injunction to the workplace and attempted to narrow the scope of the injunction via a proposed list of specific words that the district court could ban. Not satisfied that these modifications made the injunction comport with the First Amendment, Avis appealed to the California Supreme Court.

Federal courts have expressed alarm at hostile environment law's growing conflict with freedom of speech.

A four-to-three majority of the state supreme court upheld the appellate court's decision. The three dissenters argued that the injunction amounted to a prior restraint on constitutionally protected speech. They pointed out that U.S. Supreme Court precedent shows that prior restraints are not allowed for speech that might, but won't necessarily, be illegal. The reason for this rule is that such restraints have a chilling effect on what could have been legal, protected speech. For example, a single future pejorative use of a racial epithet, although banned by the injunction, cannot be the severe and pervasive harassment required to create an illegal hostile work environment; in some contexts it might be severe, but a single comment cannot be "pervasive." For that matter, racial epithets can be uttered in contexts that do not evince hostility. For example, epithets could be mentioned during "diversity education" or could be used ironically, yet these uses of the epithets would be equally banned by the injunction's prior restraint. Justice Clarence Thomas urged his colleagues to hear Avis's appeal to the U. S. Supreme Court because of the "troubling free speech issues" raised by the case, but he was not successful, and the injunction stood.

The Future of Workplace Harassment Law

The ultimate outcome of the battle between the First Amendment and the speech-regulating aspects of hostile environment law thus remains unresolved and will remain that way until the Supreme Court chooses to resolve the issue. No court has yet held directly that the First Amendment prohibits workplace speech from being the basis of Title VII liability if that speech would be protected in other contexts. However, four Supreme Court justices have suggested that hostile environment law sometimes violates the First Amendment, and other federal courts have expressed alarm at hostile environment law's growing conflict with freedom of speech.

Federal courts have also been sympathetic to First Amendment objections to prophylactic measures ordered by state and local governments to avoid creating a hostile environment in the public sector workplace. For example, courts have held that prohibiting prisoners and on-duty firefighters from reading *Playboy* unconstitutionally restricts expression, despite claims that allowing pornographic magazines to be read creates a hostile work environment for female prison guards and firefighters.

The public is growing impatient with the corrosive effect of hostile environment law on freedom of expression.

In the absence of definitive Supreme Court guidance, however, hostile environment law marches on. In February 2002, for example, Anchorage, Alaska, fearing lawsuits by female firefighters, banned from its firehouse not only *Playboy* and other pornographic magazines, but also the slightly racy men's magazine *Maxim*. And the law continues to grow. The latest trend in this expansion is employees suing employers for not preventing hostile environments allegedly created by patrons. For example, the Equal Employment Opportunity Commission has declared that 12 Minneapolis librarians were subjected to a sexually hostile work environment when they were exposed to pornography accessed on the Internet by library patrons. If courts agree with the EEOC, all libraries, public and private, will need to ban Internet access to "offensive" sites or face hostile environment liability.

Public Impatience

There are signs that the public is growing impatient with the corrosive effect of hostile environment law on freedom of expression. One of the more amusing manifestations of this disquiet is an episode of the animated series *South Park*. After a visit from the "Sexual Harassment Panda," the children of South Park begin to sue each other for harassment over minor insults. Eventually, the children pursue deeper pockets, the school at which these insults take place. The school is bankrupted, while Kyle's attorney father, who represents all of the plaintiffs, becomes wealthy. This leads to the following exchange:

Father: You see, son, we live in a liberal democratic society. The Democrats [sic—it was a mostly Republican EEOC and Supreme Court] created sexual harassment law, which tells us what we can and cannot say in the workplace, and what we can and cannot do in the workplace.

Kyle: But isn't that fascism?

Father: No, because we don't call it fascism.

Speech That Criticizes Religion Should Not Be Banned

A. C. Grayling

A. C. Grayling is a professor of philosophy at the University of London.

[The British government's] efforts to reduce the risk of terrorist atrocities such as the London bombings of 7 July [2005] have two aspects. One is about enhanced security, the other is about reassuring Britain's 1.6 million Muslims that they are welcome here. The government's hearts-and-minds strategy includes funding moderate Islamic news media, encouraging the setting up of Muslim interest-exempt banking facilities, and persuading companies to set aside prayer rooms for Muslim employees. It also, much more controversially, includes the bill, currently before parliament, to criminalise incitement to religious hatred.

Because Muslims are an ethnically diverse group, they are not protected by the race laws [which forbid inciting racial hatred], and yet they have been made to feel the need for something analogous by anti-Islamic sentiment after the terrorist attacks. This is what the proposed incitement law is designed to provide. But the law is a serious mistake. Intended as a positive gesture towards a small minority of the British population, it represents a drastic step towards limiting freedom of expression for the entire population—and that is far too high a cost to pay.

Threat to Free Speech

Most countries, apart from the United States, have laws criminalising offences against religion. In the west, such laws have

A. C. Grayling, "Religious Radicals Want to Limit Our Freedoms, So to Curb Free Speech Is to Give Them Exactly What They Want," *New Statesman*, vol. 134, July 18, 2005, pp. 22–24. Copyright © 2005 New Statesman, Ltd. Reproduced by permission.

been dead letters for the past century and more, because the opposing value of free speech has been regarded as far outweighing them. However, there are sudden danger signals in secular Europe now, warning of a reversal of this arrangement. One indication is that just as the British government puts forward its religious hatred law, so a magistrate in Bergamo, Italy, is invoking an old statute criminalising vilification of religion to indict his country's most celebrated journalist—who stands charged with defaming Islam.

The threat to free speech from religion-protecting laws is so obvious that advocates of Britain's proposed statute are careful to insist that it has inbuilt free-speech safeguards. They claim that satire and criticism directed at religion will not result in prison sentences, because the law is aimed at protecting people not beliefs, and because the Director of Public Prosecutions will have a veto over proposed indictments to ensure that the law is not abused.

Are such reassurances satisfactory? Laws can change in the light of circumstance, so in harsher times this one could easily be refocused to protect against much vaguer provocations, such as offence or derogatory remarks. Consider the similarity of certain laws in present-day Pakistan to those in the not-too-distant history of Europe. A Pakistani statute of 1984 specifies life imprisonment or death for derogatory remarks about the Koran. The country's federal sharia [Islamic religious law] court additionally ruled in 1990 that the penalty for contempt of the Holy Prophet was death and nothing else. These uncompromising laws resemble those protecting Christianity in earlier phases of European history, when cognate crimes of heresy and blasphemy were capital offences. As this shows, history has a bad habit of repeating itself in different places and guises, especially if a door is left ajar for it to do so.

The Italian journalist currently in trouble is Oriana Fallaci, one of her country's most distinguished writers. If found guilty, she faces two years in prison. Since 11 September 2001 she has assumed the role of defender of western values against Islamic assaults upon them. The occasion for her indictment is a book called *The Force of Reason*, in which among other things she laments what she sees as a deliberate invasion of Europe by Muslim immigrants, who she says intend to conquer Europe and efface its culture and identity. In support of these claims, she cites a speech allegedly made by the then Algerian president Houari Boumedienne in 1974: "One day millions of men will leave the southern hemisphere to go to the northern hemisphere. And they will not go there as friends. Because they will go there to conquer it. And they will conquer it with their sons. The wombs of our women will give us victory." She quotes a Catholic bishop who allegedly heard a Muslim cleric tell westerners at an interfaith meeting in Turkey: "Thanks to your democratic laws we will invade you; thanks to our Islamic laws we will conquer you."

Threatening behavior, assault and battery have always been crimes, whatever provokes them. No new crime need be invented.

Most of Fallaci's anger is reserved for the failure of Europe to recognise what she sees as the currency of these threats. Her impassioned response to the events of 11 September, the blunt language she uses in criticising the sons of Allah [Muslims] and asserting the superiority of European liberalism over Islamic culture, has provoked an Islamist activist in Italy, one Adel Smith (an Egyptian-Scottish immigrant), to lay a complaint against her under the vilification of religion law. Ironically, Smith is himself on indictment under the same law, for abusing Catholicism; and he is well known in Italy for provocative activities, demanding that crucifixes be removed from schools and hospitals, and allegedly calling for Fallaci to be exterminated.

Existing Laws Provide Enough Protection

In circumstances where tensions are provoked by assertive identity politics based on faith affiliation, such laws provide ready weapons for all sides to attack each other in the courtroom. It is a short step from there to riots in the streets outside. Rhetoric matters in such cases; if someone is indicted for disturbing the peace rather than specifically for causing religious offence, there is far less rationale for faith groups to gather outside court-houses and brandish sticks.

Britain already has laws protecting its citizens from verbal or physical attack, no matter how motivated. A Metropolitan Police leaflet, printed in no fewer than 11 languages, asks: "Have you ever been abused or attacked because of your race, your religion, the colour of your skin, or your sexual orientation?" And it tells readers that the police can protect anyone thus abused, if appropriate, by arresting those responsible. That is unequivocal: threatening behaviour, assault and battery have always been crimes, whatever provokes them. No new crime need be invented.

The Oriana Fallaci case shows why inventing a crime would be profoundly misguided, because it illustrates the danger posed by laws that specifically protect faiths and their votaries. Fallaci's book is very blunt in its criticisms of Islam, so both its manner and its matter are controversial. The point at issue, however, is not her views; it is her right to express them.

At this juncture in history, when a new clash is occurring—or rather, being deliberately engineered—between the secular arrangements of European liberal democracies and some increasingly assertive religious groups operating within them, the need for free speech, however abrasive and challenging, is greater than ever. Religious radicals want to limit our freedoms; to curb free speech is to give them exactly what they want. The worst-case scenario is that what will come from limiting free speech is, in the end, silence.

Religion Should Not Be Treated Like Race

No one is a Christian or Muslim at birth; people are made so by the community they are born into, or which they later join. They can choose not to be Christian or Muslim, and can convert to another faith or none. But they cannot choose to be other than ethnically white or black. Ultimately, membership of a religious group is a voluntary matter—even if the coercive effects of brainwashing in childhood and social pressure to conform can make opting out of it difficult. This puts all religions on the same footing as political parties and other voluntary organisations: they are self-selected interest groups, defined by belief, aim and personal conviction. No one would tolerate the idea that members of a political party should be protected by law against criticism or satire; by the same token neither should a religion and its members.

This especially matters now, because the major religions are busily engaged in pushing themselves further into the public domain, demanding more privileges and protections there than they have enjoyed for a long time. The vacuum left by the end of the cold war has been filled by increasing Islamist militancy, premised on hostility to a materialist west, which militant leaders blame for their problems. The other major religions, not wishing to be left behind in the assertiveness stakes, make common cause with them, demanding public money for faith-based schools (the dreadful consequences of which can be seen to this day in Northern Ireland), faith representation in the House of Lords [the upper house of the British legislature], new laws protecting believers qua [as] believers, and much besides.

This common cause adopted by different religious groups can only be temporary, because each faith lays claim to the final truth and so by their nature they blaspheme one another. Deep, traditional conflicts are merely waiting for their time to reemerge, something far more likely to happen if religions have been given a larger slice of the public domain and protection for their special-interest activities there.

In this climate, whether or not one agrees with Fallaci's views, her indictment is a portent for Britain and all of Europe. It represents secularism and free speech under pressure, indeed under threat: and passing laws to give self-described believers protection from both secularism and free speech increases that pressure, and promises ultimately to turn the threat into reality.

Protests at Funerals Should Not Be Banned

Michelle Cottle

Michelle Cottle is a senior editor at the New Republic, *a weekly opinion magazine.*

Some laws seem so well-intentioned, so harmless, so utterly right-minded that you feel like a complete heel for objecting to them.

Take the recent efforts in Kansas and a handful of other Midwestern states to pass legislation banning protests at funerals. The proposed laws are a targeted, somewhat urgent move to combat the repugnant antics of a group of gay-bashing bigots so self-righteously vitriolic in their "God Hates Fags" moralizing they make [televangelist] Pat Robertson look like Carson [Kressey] from *Queer Eye.*

Anti-Gay Protests at Funerals

I refer, of course, to the Reverend Fred Phelps and some of the more devoted congregants of his Westboro Baptist Church of Topeka, Kansas. For those of you unfamiliar with Brother Phelps, he is the militant Christian soldier who for years has been leading protests—mini hate-fests, really—at gay funerals, loudly asserting that every unpleasantness to befall any citizen of this nation is divine retribution for our satanically inspired toleration of sodomites. Growing ever more unhinged with advancing age, Brother Phelps's giddy response to the atrocities of September 11—"The rod of God has smitten fag America!"—suggests a level of religious certitude that would embarrass [Muslim terrorist leader] Osama [bin Laden] himself.

Michelle Cottle, "Grave Danger," *The New Republic Online*, February 3, 2006. Reproduced by permission of The New Republic.

No longer content to target gays and their grieving loved ones, Phelps & friends have been branching out, protesting any high-profile funeral where they can pick up a bit of free media, such as memorials held for the victims of the West Virginia mining tragedy or for troops killed in Iraq. No matter whether the deceased in question were gay, or that many may well have shared Phelps's moral objection to homosexuality: as the Reverend's daughter Shirley Phelps-Roper (an attorney for Westboro no less) so elegantly articulated to *The Washington Post*, "Our goal is to call America an abomination, to help the nation connect the dots. You turn this nation over to the fags and our soldiers come home in body bags."

Outraged legislators in states near Phelps's base of operations are looking for a way to end this harassment of grieving war widows and orphans. Kansas, unsurprisingly, is leading the charge: With one apparently vague, hard-to-enforce law prohibiting funeral protests already on the books, the state is looking to toughen its stance by barring demonstrators from coming within 300 feet of any funeral or memorial service and prohibiting demonstrations for one hour before and two hours after such services. Indiana lawmakers, meanwhile, want to make protesting within 500 feet of a funeral a felony punishable by up to three years in prison and a $10,000 fine. Similar proposals are being entertained in Illinois, Missouri, and Oklahoma.

Not every ugly word or hateful poster is a threat.

Considering the depravity of what Brother Phelps and his merry band of hatemongers are doing, such legislative restraining efforts are completely understandable—admirable even. Unfortunately, they are also misguided and ultimately injurious to all of us.

Infantilizing Americans

Now I'm no [Supreme Court] Justice [Samuel] Alito and as such have no intention of engaging in a constitutional throw-down about the First Amendment rights of homophobic whackjobs. (Besides, who wants to sound like an ACLU [American Civil Liberties Union] fanatic?) But free-speech issues aside, I think we need to avoid doing anything more to promote the idea that the best and only way for our society to express its disapproval of a particular behavior is to outlaw it. Likewise, we need to stop feeding the notion that we the people are so very fragile and delicate in our sensibilities that the only way we know how to handle the uglier aspects of life is to call in the state to make them go away.

Americans are supposed to be self-sufficient, spunky, strong-willed, independent types. So why is it that any time some drooling imbecile wolf-whistles at a gal on the street, or a drunk frat boy tosses off a racial slur, or some Bible thumper starts ranting about how all gays, Jews, feminists, Frenchmen, Anabaptists, and recovering [John] Kerry voters are on the fast track to hell, we start speed dialing our congressmen about drafting a bill to ban Behavior X? Then we phone our lawyer to see if a civil suit is possible. As dangerously frail and legalistic as this nation is becoming, it's only a matter of time before someone decides that the future of the republic is in peril unless we immediately pass a constitutional amendment banning trash talk at basketball games.

Before anyone starts freaking out, let me clarify that I'm all for laws that prevent the flagrant abuse of power, such as in superior-subordinate interactions in the workplace, school, military, etc. Nor am I arguing in defense of stalking or other truly menacing behavior.

But not every ugly word or hateful poster is a threat. And by larding the list of legally proscribed behavior, we run the risk of infantilizing the entire populace, of convincing ourselves that the state is responsible for shielding us from any and all unpleasantness. With that operating philosophy, we might as well invite the NSA [National Security Agency] to tap all our phone lines to make sure none of us is bothered by an obscene caller ever again.

Mature Responses to Hateful Speech

Instead, we need to put a little more energy into figuring out how to deal with things that make us unhappy without calling in Big Brother. Case in point: I was intrigued and more than a little moved by one countermeasure to Phelps already being practiced by a bunch of biker vets known as the Patriot Guard. At the behest of service members' families, the group has begun attending the funerals of the fallen to serve as a buffer between the mourners and the nutters. Is this solution as tidy as having a row of police officers barring Phelps from the premises? Probably not. Then again, there's always the delightful possibility that Phelps will accidentally become entangled in the spokes of someone's Harley Road King.

Kidding aside, much like skinheads and Louis Farrakhan [leader of the Nation of Islam, an organization of African American Muslims] and Dr. Phil and any other number of corrosive gasbags I wouldn't mind seeing slathered in honey and staked out on a hill of fire ants, Fred Phelps should be allowed to peddle his brand of insanity in even the most inappropriate venues. Because even if you're not worried about the Constitution, you should be worried about our individual constitutions. Americans need to stop inviting our government to treat us like children—particularly with the current government, which already behaves a bit too father-knows-bestish for many people's taste. Sadly, this means that irretrievably wicked or congenitally stupid people sometimes succeed in upsetting perfectly decent folk. But that is the price of being a nation of grown-ups.

CHAPTER 2

Should High Schools and Universities Censor?

Chapter Preface

The first Supreme Court decision to declare that students had First Amendment rights while inside their schools was handed down on February 24, 1969. On that day the Supreme Court ruled in favor of three Iowa students—siblings John and Mary Beth Tinker and Christopher Eckhardt—and against the Des Moines Community Independent School District, which had suspended the students for protesting against the Vietnam War.

On December 11, 1965, dozens of students met at Eckhardt's home to organize an anti war protest. They decided to carry out this protest by wearing black armbands for two weeks, from December 16, 1965, through January 1, 1966. The Des Moines school district heard about their planned protest and made a new rule banning students from wearing armbands in the district's high schools. Students who defied the ban and wore armbands anyway would be suspended from school. This regulation was necessary to maintain order in the schools, school administrators claimed. The Vietnam War was very controversial, and the administrators worried that the presence of students wearing armbands to protest it would disrupt classes.

The school's ban caused many students to drop out of the protest. Some of them were worried that a suspension on their record might make it hard for them to get into college. Only Eckhardt, the Tinkers, and around twenty other students decided to carry on. Five students, including Eckhardt and the Tinkers, were suspended as a result.

Two of the suspended students gave in at that point, but the Tinkers and Eckhardt sued the school district for violating their right to free speech. The first court to hear their case dismissed it, saying that the school had a right to ban speech and actions that would disturb discipline in the schools. The students appealed and eventually the Supreme Court agreed to hear their case. The Court ruled that schools could ban speech that "materially and substantially interfere[d] with the requirements of appropriate discipline," but "undifferentiated fear or apprehension of disturbance is not enough to overcome the right to freedom of expression. . . . Any word spoken, in class, in the lunchroom, or on the campus, that deviates from the views of another person may start an argument or cause a disturbance. But our Constitution says we must take this risk."

Despite the Supreme Court's decision in 1969, many questions remain about the proper balance between the First Amendment rights of students and other competing rights. These are the questions debated by the authors in the following chapter.

High Schools Are Permitted to Ban Speech That Attacks Other Students

Stephen Reinhardt

Stephen Reinhardt is a judge on the United States Court of Appeals for the Ninth Circuit.

EDITOR'S NOTE: *The following viewpoint is an excerpt from a Ninth Circuit Court of Appeals decision,* Harper v. Poway Unified School District, *given on April 20, 2006, which affirms a lower court's ruling that Poway High School did not violate a student's right to freedom of speech.*

May a public high school prohibit students from wearing T-shirts with messages that condemn and denigrate other students on the basis of their sexual orientation? Appellant [the person bringing the appeal] in this action is a sophomore at Poway High School who was ordered not to wear a T-shirt to school that read, "BE ASHAMED, OUR SCHOOL EMBRACED WHAT GOD HAS CONDEMNED" handwritten on the front, and "HOMOSEXUALITY IS SHAMEFUL" handwritten on the back.

Factual Background

Poway High School ("the School") has had a history of conflict among its students over issues of sexual orientation. In 2003, the School permitted a student group called the Gay-Straight Alliance to hold a "Day of Silence" at the School which, in the words of an Assistant Principal, is intended to "teach tolerance of others, particularly those of a different sexual orientation." During the days surrounding the 2003 "Day of Silence," a series of incidents and altercations occurred on the school campus as a result of anti-homosexual

Stephen Reinhardt, *Harper v. Poway Unified School District*, United States Court of Appeals for the Ninth Circuit, April 20, 2006.

comments that were made by students. One such confrontation required the Principal to separate students physically. According to David LeMaster, a teacher at Poway, several students were suspended as a result of these conflicts. Moreover, a week or so after the "Day of Silence," a group of heterosexual students informally organized a "Straight-Pride Day," during which they wore T-shirts which displayed derogatory remarks about homosexuals. According to Assistant Principal Lynell Antrim, some students were asked to remove the shirts and did so, while others "had an altercation and were suspended for their actions."

Because of these conflicts in 2003, when the Gay-Straight Alliance sought to hold another "Day of Silence" in 2004, the School required the organization to consult with the Principal to "problem solve" and find ways to reduce tensions and potential altercations. On April 21, 2004, the date of the 2004 "Day of Silence," appellant Tyler Chase Harper wore a T-shirt to school on which "I WILL NOT ACCEPT WHAT GOD HAS CONDEMNED," was handwritten on the front and "HOMOSEXUALITY IS SHAMEFUL 'Romans 1:27'" was handwritten on the back. There is no evidence in the record that any school staff saw Harper's T-shirt on that day.

The next day, April 22, 2004, Harper wore the same T-shirt to school, except that the front of the shirt read "BE ASHAMED, OUR SCHOOL EMBRACED WHAT GOD HAS CONDEMNED," while the back retained the same message as before, "HOMOSEXUALITY IS SHAMEFUL 'Romans 1:27.'" LeMaster, Harper's second-period teacher, noticed Harper's shirt and observed "several students off-task talking about" the shirt. LeMaster, recalling the altercations that erupted as a result of "anti-homosexual speech" during the previous year's "Day of Silence," explained to Harper that he believed that the shirt was "inflammatory," that it violated the school's dress code, and that it "created a negative and hostile working environment for others." When Harper refused to remove his shirt and asked to speak to an administrator, LeMaster gave him a dress code violation card to take to the front office.

When Harper arrived at the front office, he met Assistant Principal Antrim. She told Harper that the "Day of Silence" was "not about the school promoting homosexuality but rather it was a student activity trying to raise other students' awareness regarding tolerance in their judgement [sic] of others." Antrim believed that Harper's shirt "was inflammatory under the circumstances and could cause disruption in the educational setting." Like LeMaster, she also recalled the altercations that had arisen as a result of anti-homosexual speech one year prior. According to her affidavit, she "discussed [with Harper] ways that he and students of his faith could bring a positive light onto this issue without the condemnation that he displayed on his shirt." Harper was informed that if he removed the shirt he could return to class.

When Harper again refused to remove his shirt, the Principal, Scott Fisher, spoke with him, explaining his concern that the shirt was "inflammatory" and that it was the school's "intent to avoid physical conflict on campus." Fisher also explained to Harper that it was not healthy for students to be addressed in such a derogatory manner. According to Fisher, Harper informed him that he had already been "confronted by a group of students on campus" and was "involved in a tense verbal conversation" earlier that morning. The Principal eventually decided that Harper could not wear his shirt on campus, a decision that, he asserts, was influenced by "the fact that during the previous year, there was tension on campus surrounding the Day of Silence between certain gay and straight students." Fisher proposed some alternatives to wearing the shirt, all of which Harper turned down. Harper asked two times to be suspended. Fisher "told him that [he] did not want him suspended from school, nor did [he] want him to have something in his disciplinary record because of a stance he felt strongly about." Instead, Fisher told Harper that he would be required to remain in the front office for the remainder of the school day. Harper spent the rest of the day in the school conference room doing his homework. . . . Harper was not suspended, no disciplinary record was placed in his file, and he received full attendance credit for the day.

On June 2, 2004, Harper filed a lawsuit in district court against Poway Unified School District and certain named individuals in their individual and official capacities. Harper alleged five federal causes of action—violations of his right to free speech, his right to free exercise of religion, the Establishment Clause, the Equal Protection Clause, and the Due Process Clause—and one state law claim based on California Civil Code § 52.1, which creates a private cause of action for the violation of individual federal and state constitutional rights. . . .

The First Amendment rights of students in public schools are not automatically coextensive with the rights of adults in other settings.

Student Speech Under *Tinker v. Des Moines Independent Community School District*

Public schools are places where impressionable young persons spend much of their time while growing up. They do so in order to receive what society hopes will be a fair and full education—an education without which they will almost certainly fail in later life, likely sooner rather than later. . . . The public school, with its free education, is the key to our democracy. . . . Almost all young Americans attend public schools. During the time they do—from first grade through twelfth—students are discovering what and who they are. Often, they are insecure. Generally, they are vulnerable to cruel, inhuman, and prejudiced treatment by others.

The courts have construed the First Amendment as applied to public schools in a manner that attempts to strike a balance between the free speech rights of students and the special need to maintain a safe, secure and effective learning environment. . . . This court has expressly recognized the need for such balance: "States have a compelling interest in their educational system, and a balance must be met between the First Amendment rights of students and preservation of the educational process." *LaVine v. Blaine Sch. Dist.*, 257 F.3d 981, 988 (9th Cir. 2001). Although public school students do not "shed their constitutional rights to freedom of speech or expression at the schoolhouse gate," *Tinker*, 393 U.S. at 506 (1969), the Supreme Court has declared that "the First Amendment rights of students in public schools are not automatically coextensive with the rights of adults in other settings, and must be applied in light of the special characteristics of the school environment." *Hazelwood Sch. Dist. v. Kuhlmeier*, 484 U.S. 260, 266 (1988) (internal citation and quotation marks omitted). Thus, while Harper's shirt embodies the very sort of political speech that would be afforded First Amendment protection outside of the public school setting, his rights in the case before us must be determined "in light of [those] special characteristics." *Tinker*, 393 U.S. at 506.

A school may regulate student speech that would 'impinge upon the rights of other students.'

This court has identified "three distinct areas of student speech," each of which is governed by different Supreme Court precedent: (1) vulgar, lewd, obscene, and plainly offensive speech which is governed by [*Bethel Sch. Dist. v.*] *Fraser*, (2) school-sponsored speech which is governed by *Hazelwood*, and (3) all other speech which is governed by *Tinker*. *Chandler v. McMinnville Sch. Dist.*, 978 F.2d 524, 529 (9th Cir. 1992) (internal citations omitted).

In *Tinker*, the Supreme Court confirmed a student's right to free speech in public schools. In balancing that right against the state interest in maintaining an ordered and effective public education system, however, the Court declared that a student's speech rights could be curtailed under two circumstances. First, a school may regulate student speech that would "impinge upon the rights of other students." *Tinker*, 393 U.S. at 509. Second, a school may prohibit student speech that would result in "substantial disruption of or material interference with school activities." *Id.* at 514. Because, as we explain below, the School's prohibition of the wearing of the demeaning T-shirt is constitutionally permissible under the first of the *Tinker* prongs, we conclude that the district court did not abuse its discretion in finding that Harper failed to demonstrate a likelihood of success on the merits of his free speech claim.

Public school students who may be injured by verbal assaults . . . have a right to be free from such attacks while on school campuses.

The Rights of Other Students

In *Tinker*, the Supreme Court held that public schools may restrict student speech which "intrudes upon . . . the rights of other students" or "colli[des] with the rights of other students to be secure and to be let alone." 393 U.S. at 508. Harper argues that *Tinker*'s reference to the "rights of other students" should be construed narrowly to involve only circumstances in which a student's right to be free from direct physical confrontation is infringed. Drawing on the Fifth Circuit's opinion in *Blackwell v. Issaquena County Bd. of Ed.*, 363 F.2d 749, 751 (5th Cir. 1966), which the Supreme Court cited in *Tinker*, Harper contends that because the speakers in *Blackwell* "accosted other students by pinning the buttons on them even though they did not ask for one," a student must be physically accosted in order to have his rights infringed.

Notwithstanding the facts of *Blackwell*, the law does not support Harper's argument. This court has explained that vulgar, lewd, obscene, indecent, and plainly offensive speech "by definition, may well 'impinge[] upon the rights of other students,'" even if the speaker does not directly accost individual students with his remarks. *Chandler*, 978 F.2d at 529 (quoting *Tinker*, 393 U.S. at 509). So too may other speech capable of causing psychological injury. The Tenth Circuit has held that the "display of the Confederate flag might . . . interfere with the rights of other students to be secure and let alone," even though there was no indication that any student was physically accosted with the flag, aside from its general display. *West v. Derby Unified Sch. Dist.*, 206 F.3d 1358, 1366 (10th Cir. 2000). While "[t]he precise scope of *Tinker's* 'interference with the rights of others' language is unclear," *Saxe v. State Coll. Area Sch. Dist.*, 240 F.3d 200, 217 (3rd Cir. 2001), we unequivocally reject Harper's overly narrow reading of the phrase.

We conclude that Harper's wearing of his T-shirt "colli[des] with the rights of other students" in the most fundamental way. *Tinker*, 393 U.S. at 508. Public school students who may be injured by verbal assaults on the basis of a core identifying characteristic such as race, religion, or sexual orientation, have a right to be free from such attacks while on school campuses. As *Tinker* clearly states, students have the right to "be secure and to be let alone." . . . Being secure involves not only freedom from physical assaults but from psychological attacks that cause young people to question their self-worth and their rightful place in society. The "right to be let alone" has been recognized by the Supreme Court, of course, as "'the most comprehensive of rights and the right most valued by civilized men.'" *Hill v. Colorado*, 530 U.S. 703, 716 17 (2000) (quoting *Olmstead v. United States*, 277 U.S. 438, 478 (1928) (Brandeis, J., dissenting)). Indeed, the "recognizable privacy interest in avoiding unwanted communication" is perhaps most important "when persons are 'powerless to avoid' it." *Id.* at 716 (quoting *Cohen v. California*, 403 U.S. 15, 21–22 (1971)). Because minors are subject to mandatory attendance requirements, the Court has emphasized "the obvious concern on the part of parents, and school authorities acting *in loco parentis* ['in the place of a parent'], to protect children—especially in a captive audience. . . ." *Fraser*, 478 U.S. at 684. Although name-calling is ordinarily protected outside the school context, "[s]tudents cannot hide behind the First Amendment to protect their 'right' to abuse and intimidate other students at school." *Sypniewski v. Warren Hills Reg'l Bd. of Educ.*, 307 F.3d 243, 264 (3rd Cir. 2002).

Harm to Members of Oppressed Groups

Speech that attacks high school students who are members of minority groups that have historically been oppressed, subjected to verbal and physical abuse, and made to feel inferior, serves to injure and intimidate them, as well as to damage their sense of security and interfere with their opportunity to learn. The demeaning of young gay and lesbian students in a school environment is detrimental not only to their psychological health and well-being, but also to their educational development. Indeed, studies demonstrate that "academic under-achievement, truancy, and dropout are prevalent among homosexual youth and are the probable consequences of violence and verbal and physical abuse at school." Susanne M. Stronski Huwiler and Gary Remafedi, *Adolescent Homosexuality*, 33 REV. JUR. U.I.P.R. 151, 164 (1999). . . . In short, it is well established that attacks on students on the basis of their sexual orientation are harmful not only to the students' health and welfare, but also to their educational performance and their ultimate potential for success in life.

Those who administer our public educational institutions need not tolerate verbal assaults that may destroy the self-esteem of our most vulnerable teenagers and interfere with their educational development. . . . To the contrary, the school had a valid and lawful basis for restricting Harper's wearing of his T-shirt on the ground that his conduct was injurious to gay and lesbian students and interfered with their right to learn. . . .

Student Speech That May Not Be Banned

In his declaration in the district court, the school principal justified his actions on the basis that "any shirt which is worn on campus which speaks in a derogatory manner towards an individual or group of individuals is not healthy for young people. . . ." If, by this, the principal meant that all such shirts may be banned under *Tinker*, we do not agree. T-shirts proclaiming, "Young Republicans Suck," or "Young Democrats Suck," for example, may not be very civil but they would certainly not be sufficiently damaging to the individual or the educational process to warrant a limitation on the wearer's First Amendment rights. Similarly, T-shirts that denigrate the President, his administration, or his policies, or otherwise invite political disagreement or debate, including debates over the war in Iraq, would not fall within the "rights of others" *Tinker* prong.

Although we hold that the School's restriction of Harper's right to carry messages on his T-shirt was permissible under *Tinker*, we reaffirm the importance of preserving student speech about controversial issues generally and protecting the bedrock principle that students "may not be confined to the expression of those sentiments that are officially approved." *Tinker*, 393 U.S. at 511. . . . It is essential that students have the opportunity to engage in full and open political expression, both in and out of the school environment. Engaging in controversial political speech, even when it is offensive to others, is an important right of all Americans and learning the value of such freedoms is an essential part of a public school education. Indeed, the inculcation of "the fundamental values necessary to the maintenance of a democratic political system" is "truly the 'work of the schools.'" *Fraser*, 478 U.S. at 683 (quoting *Tinker*, 393 U.S. at 508). Limitations on student speech must be narrow, and applied with sensitivity and for reasons that are consistent with the fundamental First Amendment mandate. Accordingly, we limit our holding to instances of derogatory and injurious remarks directed at students' minority status such as race, religion, and sexual orientation. Moreover, our decision is based not only on the type and degree of injury the speech involved causes to impressionable young people, but on the locale in which it takes place. . . . Thus, it is limited to conduct that occurs in public high schools (and in elementary schools). As young students acquire more strength and maturity, and specifically as they reach college age, they become adequately equipped emotionally and intellectually to deal with the type of verbal assaults that may be prohibited during their earlier years. Accordingly, we do not condone the use in public colleges or other public institutions of higher learning of restrictions similar to those permitted here.

A school may prohibit student speech . . . if the speech violates the rights of others or is materially disruptive.

Finally, we emphasize that the school's actions here were no more than necessary to prevent the intrusion on the rights of other students. Aside from prohibiting the wearing of the shirt, the school did not take the additional step of punishing the speaker: Harper was not suspended from school nor was the incident made a part of his disciplinary record.

Under the circumstances present here, we conclude that the school's actions did not extend beyond the scope of the restrictions permitted by *Tinker*. . . .

Viewpoint Discrimination

In reaching our decision that Harper may lawfully be prohibited from wearing his T-shirt, we reject his argument that the school's action constituted impermissible viewpoint discrimination. The government is generally prohibited from regulating speech "when the specific motivating ideology or the opinion or perspective of the speaker is the rationale for the restriction." *Rosenberger*, 515 U.S. at 829. However, as the district court correctly pointed out, speech in the public schools is not always governed by the same rules that apply in other circumstances. . . . Indeed, the Court in *Tinker* held that a school may prohibit student speech, even if the consequence is viewpoint discrimination, if the speech violates the rights of other students or is materially disruptive. . . . Thus, pursuant to *Tinker*, courts have allowed schools to ban the display of Confederate flags despite the fact that such a ban may constitute viewpoint discrimination. . . . While the Confederate flag may express a particular viewpoint, "[i]t is not only constitutionally allowable for school officials" to limit the expression of racially explosive views, "it is their duty to do so." *Scott*, 324 F.3d at 1249. Because, as we have already explained, the record demonstrates that Harper's speech intruded upon the rights of other students, the School's restriction is permissible under *Tinker*, and we must reject Harper's viewpoint discrimination claim. . . .

"A school need not tolerate student speech that is inconsistent with its basic educational mission, [. . .] even though the government could not censor similar speech outside the school." *Hazelwood Sch. Dist. v. Kuhlmeier*, 484 U.S. 260, 266 (1988) (citation and internal quotation marks omitted). Part of a school's "basic educational mission" is the inculcation of "fundamental values of habits and manners of civility essential to a democratic society." *Fraser*, 478 U.S. at 681 (internal quotation marks omitted). For this reason, public schools may permit, and even encourage, discussions of tolerance, equality and democracy, without being required to provide equal time for student or other speech espousing intolerance, bigotry or hatred. As we have explained, ... because a school sponsors a "Day of Religious Tolerance," it need not permit its students to wear T-shirts reading, "Jews Are Christ-Killers" or "All Muslims Are Evil Doers." Such expressions would be "wholly inconsistent with the 'fundamental values' of public school education." *Id.* at 685–86. Similarly, a school that permits a "Day of Racial Tolerance," may restrict a student from displaying a swastika or a Confederate Flag. In sum, a school has the right to teach civic responsibility and tolerance as part of its basic educational mission; it need not as a quid pro quo permit hateful and injurious speech that runs counter to that mission.

We again emphasize that we do not suggest that all debate as to issues relating to tolerance or equality may be prohibited. As we have stated repeatedly, we consider here only the question of T-shirts, banners, and other similar items bearing slogans that injure students with respect to their core characteristics. Other issues must await another day.

Schools Should Ban Sexually-Harassing Speech

Bernice Resnick Sandler and Harriett M. Stonehill

Bernice Resnick Sandler is a senior scholar at the Women's Research and Education Institute. Harriet M. Stonehill is director of the MegaSkills Education Center, Home and School Institute. The two collaborated to write Student-to-Student Sexual Harassment K–12: Strategies and Solutions for Educators to Use in the Classroom, School, and Community, *from which the following viewpoint is excerpted.*

[Examples of sexually harassing behavior include the following anecdotes:]

- "Today, as usual, I observed sexist behavior in my art class. Boys taunting girls and girls taunting boys has become a real problem. I wish they would all stop yelling at each other so that for once I could have art class in peace. This is my daily list of words I heard today that could be taken as sexual harassment: bitch, hooker, pimp, whore."

- Every day for many months, when the girl went to school she was surrounded by a group of boys who called her "a cow," an allusion to her large breasts, and would make "mooing" sounds to her. Sometimes they would follow her around, saying the same things again and again.

- Both boys and girls compile "slam books" that name and rate students in negative sexual terms such as "biggest slut," "worst in bed," "ugliest girl," or "biggest prude." Girls are often called "whore" or "slut," and boys are often called "faggot" or "condom seller." Sexual harassment is unacceptable. It is unacceptable in the workplace, and it is unacceptable in school. Students should not fear for their lives or safety on school grounds, nor should they be in fear of being bullied or harassed.

What Is Sexual Harassment?

Sexual harassment is any form of *unwanted sexual behavior* that makes students feel uncomfortable and unsafe, so that they are often unable to focus on learning, studying, working, achieving, or participating in school activities. . . . It is a form of bullying, where one student attempts to intimidate another student by using sexuality as a weapon. This unwelcome behavior is verbal, physical, or both, and occurs between boys and girls and between students of the same gender. Sometimes it involves a group of students harassing others. It also includes harassment of lesbian and gay students.

Although teachers, students, and parents typically recognize bullying behavior, they are less likely to recognize or acknowledge peer sexual harassment. Many adults fail to recognize this behavior as sexual harassment when it occurs among students. Student-to-student sexual harassment is prohibited under law; bullying is not. Although some schools offer "bullying prevention programs," they often fail to include sexual harassment as a form of bullying.

What Kinds of Behavior Are Considered to Be Sexual Harassment?

Sexual harassment covers a wide range of behaviors such as the following:

- Sexual intimidation by word or action

- Sexualized insults and name-calling, such as calling girls "sluts," "whores," "cows," "pussies," or "lesbians," or calling boys "fags" and "pussies"

- Sexual graffiti in places such as bathrooms, cafeterias, hallways, stairwells, on desks and tables, on lockers, and in outdoor areas

- Pictures or displays of sexually suggestive objects, or other materials

- Suggestive cartoons, pornography

- Pulling down a student's pants, flipping up skirts, or snapping bras

- Sexualized remarks or off-color jokes

- Circulating lists describing alleged sexual attributes or activities of students

- Spreading sexual rumors about students

- Unwanted phone calls, e-mail, regular mail, or notes about sexuality or that are obscene and/or threatening

- Pressure for sexual activity

- Teasing about a student's sexual activities or lack of sexual activity (Note: teasing can sometimes be a form of affectionate play between individuals but it can also be a form of humiliation and intimidation.). . .

Sexual harassment and bullying are unwanted behaviors by their victims. Both involve a difference in power—the power of one peer over another. Boys often have more physical power than girls; a group of harassers is more powerful than its single target; popular students have more social power than others. These differences in power are exhibited in boy/girl, girl/boy, boy/boy, and girl/girl sexual harassment.

Although not all bullying is sexual harassment, most sexual harassment is a form of bullying. Both bullying and sexual harassment intimidate, both are a form of aggression, and both have the potential to harm both the victim and the person committing the aggression. . . .

Student conduct that disrupts class work is not protected by the Constitutional right to free speech.

Is Sexual Harassment Illegal?

Not only is student-to-student harassment painful and an impediment to student learning and development, it is prohibited by several laws and regulations:

- Title IX of the Education Amendments of 1972 prohibits sex discrimination in schools receiving federal dollars. Under Title IX schools can be held liable for monetary damages *if* they know that sexual harassment exists *and if* they are "deliberately indifferent" to it *and* the harassment is so severe, pervasive, and objectively offensive that it effectively affects the student's access to an educational opportunity or benefit. (In *Davis v. Monroe County Board of Education* the U.S. Supreme Court confirmed that Title IX's prohibition of sex discrimination includes student-to-student sexual harassment.). . .

- State civil laws, such as those prohibiting sex discrimination in schools, may apply. Some states have "little Title IX" laws much like the federal Title IX law whose antidiscrimination provisions would similarly prohibit student-to-student sexual harassment. Some states have enacted anti-bullying statutes that might also prohibit student-to-student sexual harassment. Other state civil laws may also prohibit student-to-student sexual harassment. . . .

- Protections stated in the U.S. Constitution may apply in some instances to harassment based on sex and sexual orientation.

- Additional federal, state, or local laws may also apply when other forms of discrimination (such as those based on disability, race, color, national origin, and sexual orientation) are combined with sexual harassment.

- Federal, state, or local laws prohibiting "hate crimes" may also apply. . . .

- Tort laws such as those covering "negligence" and "intentional infliction of emotional harm" have been used in peer harassment cases.

- State or local laws may prohibit discrimination on the basis of sexual orientation.

- State Board of Education rules and regulations that cover reporting of sexual abuse and assault and those that prohibit sexual harassment, including harassment on the basis of sexual orientation, may also apply. Stopping sexual harassment when it occurs can often prevent a lawsuit against a school district. Districts are usually sued not because one student has sexually harassed another but because a school allowed the sexually harassing behavior to continue and ignored the fact that the children were being hurt and needed help.

Free Speech and Sexual Harassment

Sometimes students and staff erroneously believe that everyone has a right to free speech so that even sexually harassing conduct can be justified by and upheld by the Constitution.

Although freedom of speech as guaranteed by the Constitution applies to both written and oral speech, the right to free speech is not an absolute one—especially when a school is disrupted, a student's rights have been violated, or a threat has been made. For example, the U.S. Supreme Court has ruled that student conduct that disrupts class work is not protected by the Constitutional right to free speech. "[C]onduct by the student, in class or out of it, which for any reason—whether it stems from time, place or type of behavior—materially disrupts class work or involves substantial disorder or invasion of the rights of others is, of course, not immunized by the constitutional guarantee of freedom of speech."

In another case, involving sexual innuendos in a student's speech to a school assembly, the Supreme Court stated that "the constitutional rights of students in public school are not automatically coextensive with the rights of adults in other settings."

Additionally, the Supreme Court has upheld a principal's decision to remove two articles from a student newspaper when the "free speech" involved has the school's imprimatur.

Freedom of speech generally applies to e-mail and the Internet in the same way as it applies to other forms of speech. Thus students' use of school computers to post sexually offensive or harassing materials can be prohibited by schools just as a school may prohibit lewd or vulgar speech on school grounds. A key issue in incidents occurring on and off school grounds is whether these incidents caused substantial disruption.

Sexual Harassment Can Cost Schools Money

Schools are ultimately responsible for protecting children and culpable when they do not protect them.

> Katy Lyle's brother first told her about the sexual graffiti about her in the boy's bathroom of their high school. Her mother complained more than a dozen times to the school, requesting that it be removed. Despite promises to remove it, the graffiti remained for sixteen months (including two summers and Katy's entire junior year), increasing in vul-

garity, including pornographic references to dogs and accusations that Katy was having sexual relations with her brother. As the graffiti increased, classmates put obscene drawings on her desk; others sent notes demanding sex with her; still others ridiculed her, such as the boy who yelled aloud at the school's crowded entrance hall, "Hey Katy, I took a [expletive] in your stall this morning." Even after the graffiti was finally removed, Katy still shut herself into her room to cry. Her parents brought one of the first student-to-student sexual harassment cases in the United States, filing charges with the Minnesota Department of Human Rights in 1989. The case was settled for $15,000.

Tawnya Brawdy faced a gauntlet of boys for years who would gather around her and "moo" at her, calling her a cow. The taunting continued before school, during classes, during lunch throughout her high school years. When she asked the school for help, her teacher told her she would just have to put up with it. When the U.S. Department of Education investigated the complaint, they described it in a 211-page report. Brawdy sued her school district and received $20,000 in an out-of-court settlement. . . .

In Petaluma, a middle school girl was called "slut" and "hot dog bitch" and other names by her classmates who also threatened to beat her and on one occasion slapped her face. Despite her repeated complaints to the school and some disciplinary action, the harassment continued. School officials were alleged to have said that "boys will be boys" and that eventually the harassers would mature and the harassment would stop. The case was settled for $250,000.

The sixth grader in a California elementary school in Antioch was subjected to obscene gestures, demeaning comments about her body, and a near-daily barrage of vulgar verbal insults and violent threats by one of her male classmates. When the school did not respond to the parents' complaints, they went to court. A jury awarded the girl and her family $500,000. The child's father said the lawsuit had cost him most of the family's savings, about $150,000. . . .

Why Does Sexual Harassment Happen?

Students may be exploring their sexuality, and some may be unsure how to behave. They may be imitating behaviors they have seen at home, on computers or television, in movies or videos.

> By the age of nineteen our children have spent nearly 19,000 hours in front of television (compared with only 16,000 hours in school), and nearly two-thirds of all television programming has sexual content. Between 1998 and 1999, the number of sexual references on television more than tripled.

> On many sitcoms, sexual harassment is not only commonplace, but typically presented in a manner that makes it seem acceptable. In one study, 36 percent of the sexually harassing behavior was welcomed by the target of the behavior; in 24 percent of the incidents there was no visible reaction, and in 40 percent the targets did not welcome the behavior. The behaviors seem acceptable because they are accompanied by laugh tracks and there are no consequences for the person who initiated the harassing behavior. In none of the incidents was anyone sanctioned or told that a behavior was out of line.

Some students are deliberately trying to intimidate or humiliate another student. They may need to feel "powerful," and sexually harassing someone makes them feel stronger, bigger, and better than their victims. Others are imitating their peers who are harassing or may go along with their friends who harass because they are frightened of losing their friendship. Some students believe that sexually harassing behavior is the way sexuality is "normally" expressed or is a way to confirm their own sexuality. However, sexual harassment is less about sexuality than an assertion of dominance.

Some students harass weaker students because they have learned to relate to others primarily by intimidation. Others use sexual harassment to get attention from other students.

Students who engage in harassing behaviors typically learn that sexual bullying pays off. They begin to believe that relationships between men and women are based on the power to hurt another person. They are learning destructive ways of relating to their peers, exhibiting behaviors that are not only illegal but also harmful to themselves and others. All of these behaviors limit the harasser's ability to develop lifelong positive social skills and can have a serious impact on their future behavior at college, at work, and in personal relationships.

Sexual Harassment Affects All Students

Girls are more likely to be harassed than boys. Girls are typically harassed because of their appearance. "Unattractive" or "unstylish" girls as well as girls who are physically mature are at higher risk. Girls of color may be at higher risk than other girls.

Boys are often harassed by boys as well as by girls. Typically, boys are harassed because of how they behave. Boys who do not fit the stereotypic male image are more likely to be harassed and called names such as "fag," "queer," "sissy." Those who do not excel in athletics are often targets. Male-to-male sexual harassment is often not seen as sexual harassment, or if noticed, the sexual aspects are ignored and the behavior is more likely to be called bullying.

Students for whom English is a second language and *students who are small or very shy* as well as *students who are being bullied* are also more likely to be sexually harassed.

Disabled girls are also at risk. Disabled students are often unable to protect themselves either verbally or physically. Thus, they are more vulnerable to sexually harassing behaviors.

Students who are harassed may exhibit:

- Fear of coming to school—they may avoid classes or certain areas of school

- Fear of the person(s) harassing them

- Inability to concentrate or learn

- Angry feelings and behavior

- Confused feelings

- Physical symptoms such as insomnia, headaches, stomachaches, and loss of appetite

- Feelings of being isolated from other children and subsequent withdrawal from social interactions

- Blaming oneself for the harassment

- Feelings of shame about sexuality

- Feelings of humiliation

- Feelings of worthlessness, vulnerability, and anxiety

- Depression—some children have contemplated or attempted suicide.

Students who fail to get support from school and/or parents are at even greater risk for depression, isolation from peers and family, and suicidal thoughts.

The impact of being sexually harassed is long-lasting and often leaves permanent scars.

Sometimes alcohol, drug abuse, and smoking can be a reaction to sexual harassment.

Adults who have been bullied remember feeling angry, upset, frustrated, and fearful. Students who are sexually harassed have the same feelings. The impact of being sexually harassed is long-lasting and often leaves permanent scars; victims of sexual harassment often need counseling and guidance. The motivation to learn can be damaged when a student has to constantly deal with sexual harassment at school. Fear can make a student feel that he or she does not "belong."

> Someone said that I was a slut. You always try to pretend that what people say about you doesn't affect you, but it does. You slowly start to believe what's being said about you. (teenage girl)

Girls are more likely to gain a reputation of "slut" and being sexually available than boys. "A reputation acquired in young adolescence can damage a woman's self-esteem for years no matter how smart or talented she is. She may become a target for other forms of sexual harassment. She may be raped. She may become promiscuous, figuring she might as well do what she is accused of doing. Or she may shut down her sexual side entirely, wearing baggy clothes and sticking close to home."

> I really think sexual harassment can hurt because sometimes people may tease you about your body parts and it really hurts your feelings because you can't change them in any way. It can also interfere with your schoolwork because all your thoughts are on your anger and then you can't concentrate. If I am harassed in the future, I will stand up for my rights and if a teacher doesn't care, I will pressure him or her to punish my harasser.

Students who are not harassed but see it happening to others also feel vulnerable and fear that they will be the next victim. Some may even be wary of showing sympathy to those who are harassed. Acceptance of peer sexual harassment by victims and bystanders can set the stage for future sexual abuse and assault by "teaching" students that sexual hostility is "normal" and acceptable.

Ten Myths About Student-to-Student Sexual Harassment

1. *"Sexual harassment is just part of normal development. It's part of growing up."*

While it is true that often youngsters test out behaviors, they need to learn which of these behaviors are unacceptable. When students are allowed to engage in hurtful behaviors they are not learning the skills they need for life.

2. *"Normal boy-girl relationships are not allowed anymore. All this stuff about sexual harassment gets in the way of boys and girls learning to relate to each other in a friendly manner."*

Unwanted sexual innuendos, lewd comments, grabbing, and touching are not expressions of friendship nor are they the type of social relationships that students should be having with each other. Flirting and sexual harassment are very different behaviors. In flirting, the behavior is welcomed and is characterized by the respect each has for the other. Either person can stop the flirting, unlike sexual harassment. Flirting makes people feel good; harassment makes them feel bad. Often the purpose of sexual harassment is deliberate humiliation or embarrassment.

3. *"Girls get sexually harassed because they are asking for it. If they wouldn't dress provocatively we would not have a problem with sexual harassment."*

Sexual harassment can happen to anyone, no matter how they dress. The way students dress does not give someone else permission to touch them, make lewd comments, or otherwise harass them. Sexual harassment has much more to do with power and the use of sexuality to intimidate than with sexual attractiveness or appearance. Focusing on girls' clothing puts the responsibility on girls rather than on the student doing the harassing.

4. *"Sexual harassment only happens to girls."*

Although girls are more likely to be harassed, boys too can be harassed both by girls and other boys. Girls are sometimes harassed by other girls.

5. *"If students would just say 'No' or just ignore sexual harassment, it would stop."*

Saying "No" or "I want you to stop that" doesn't work all the time. Many boys believe that girls really like their behavior and believe that girls don't really mean it when they say "No." Thus a girl's "no" often becomes justification for continuing the sexual harassment. In most instances, ignoring harassment does not stop it. Indeed, the harassment may actually get worse. Not responding is often viewed as either "she likes what I said" or "she is too weak to stop me."

6. *"Sexual harassment is no big deal. People who complain usually don't have a sense of humor or don't know how to accept a compliment."*

Sexually intimidating behavior is not a compliment nor is it funny. Harassment is often painful and frightening. No one should have to accept sexual humiliation with a smile. Harassing comments about one's sexuality make many students very uncomfortable.

7. *"Sexual harassment is often unintentional."*

Whether the person meant to harass someone else is not relevant. The behavior is just as hurtful whether it is intentional or not.

8. *"Learning how to handle these behaviors will make students stronger."*

Sexual harassment does not make people stronger; in fact, it makes students feel weak, powerless, and sometimes angry. It can have life-long negative impact. We do not tolerate sexual harassment in adults or expect them to be able to deal with it on their own. Should we expect children to do so or to tolerate behaviors we do not tolerate in adults?

9. *"It's just the way boys show they like girls."*

The assumption that hurtful behavior is an *acceptable* way of showing affection sets up males and females for future abusive relationships. *No one should have to endure hurtful behavior.*

19. *"The law has gone too far. Boys and girls can get in trouble for almost anything."*

The Supreme Court, in a Title IX case, was very careful in applying the term *sexual harassment* to student misconduct. The behavior has to be so severe, pervasive, and objectively offensive that it effectively deprives the harassed student of access to educational opportunities. However, even if the behavior does not breach the law, sexually harassing behavior should not be tolerated in any school.

School Libraries Should Restrict Students' Access to Controversial Books

Mike Masterson

Mike Masterson is a staff writer for the Arkansas Democrat-Gazette.

Laurie Taylor didn't set out to become a controversial public figure.

Yet, before she could say "hardcore porn made available to my young daughter," her concerns over sexually inappropriate books in Fayetteville's school libraries had made her an easy target. And now, this pixie-like and articulate Christian mother says she has been labeled by authentic extremists as everything from a "homophobe to a bigot, a vile pig and even a Nazi." The truth that few seem to understand is that she is, plain and simple, a reasonable, devoted mother who wants only to maintain informed and effective parental influence over her two children, ages 11 and 12. And despite suffering sustained public attacks, she's never advocated banning even one of the books she finds so appalling for children. Heck, she hasn't even asked that kids be prevented from reading them. Most excerpts I've seen from these publications amount to pornographic titillation the likes of which *Hustler* magazine might proudly publish.

Before I go any further and before you explode from indignant self-righteousness, read a few excerpts for yourself at wpaag.org. Decide if you'd want your children being provided this material without your knowledge at public school. Ask yourself whether a teacher would be dismissed for reading this same material aloud in class to seventh-graders. Ask whether your own child would be suspended for reading it aloud in a cafeteria. Inform yourself.

Parents Have the Right to Choose What Their Children Read

I admire Laurie, a former U.S. Navy diver. Her cause is selfless and noble. She has had the gall to insist that parents of all elementary, middle and high school–age children actually be informed when their children check out one of the more than 70 books that concern her. These would be books that speak in grossly inappropriate terms about promiscuous romps of all imaginable shapes and forms, including incest with both parents.

This outspoken taxpayer is asking for two simple things. First, she wants these books, many by the same repetitive-message authors, placed in a restricted section of the library. Then she wants the school to notify parents and get their consent when their children seek access to one of these books either in person or by an Internet request. That's it. Period. So just what, in this age of Internet filters and parental-consent for X-rated videogames and rental movies, is so "censoring" about that? What about that makes her a Nazi or a "Christian extremist"?

Someone had to decide which books would and wouldn't be included in the school library, right? Wasn't that process a form of censorship?

This issue is not remotely about one's religious or political beliefs or one's stance on constitutional rights. It is only about a parent's right to rear children in the way he or she believes is best without the state providing hidden, potentially corrupting influences.

What we really are talking about here is sheer common sense, providing information and one woman's refusal to bend or allow corruption of the moral values that she and her husband Mark have established in their home. That's un-American?

Nonetheless, Laurie finds herself standing at ground zero in the ongoing dispute with the Fayetteville School Board over how these exploitative books should be handled.

She has been vilified as some kind of anti-First Amendment subhuman bent on burning any anti-Christian books with which she disagrees. This is utter nonsense, a diversion from the real issue at hand. Meet her yourself. Invite her to your civic club. You will see.

Adults Should Use Good Judgment About What Kids Read

After reading excerpts of this "literature," which advocates open sex of various forms with no regard for potentially disastrous health and social consequences, I found myself wondering who initially selected these books as appropriate for children. Since no school library can offer every book published, the entire process of stocking one becomes a matter of priorities. Someone had to decide which books would and wouldn't be included in the school library, right? Wasn't that process a form of censorship?

I'd venture to say that 99.999 percent of parents and grandparents and citizens wouldn't want their 11-year-olds being exposed to the shock-slop I was reading earlier this week. Just because I might write a less than mediocre book that exploits the F word for gross shock value every other sentence and describes every possible sexual activity in detail doesn't mean it has to be available to kids on library shelves in the Fayetteville public school system, does it?

Do you think I could or would publish columns that spew expletives and celebrate promiscuity and deviant sexual behavior just to shock you? No, I wouldn't, and the paper wouldn't allow it. So does that mean I am censored from freely expressing myself? No, it means I'm expected to exercise proper judgment and responsibility in the way I express my views, especially where impressionable children are concerned. I will never condone book banning. Neither will Gulf War–era vet Laurie Taylor. Yes, I am well aware of the "slippery slope" arguments that are raised when humans try to restrict free expression. But there also have to be logical boundaries in our society. And I'm one who dearly values common sense as well as decency and taste when it comes to drawing reasonable lines for our children's sake.

High Schools Should Not Ban Speech That Offends Other Students

Eugene Volokh

Eugene Volokh is a professor of law at the University of California–Los Angeles.

Sorry, your viewpoint is excluded from First Amendment protection.

That's what the Ninth Circuit [held on April 20, 2006,] as to student speech in K–12 schools, in a remarkable—and in my view deeply unsound—decision (*Harper v. Poway Unified School Dist.*).

Harper v. Poway Unified School District

Tyler Harper wore an anti-homosexuality T-shirt to school, apparently responding to a pro-gay-rights event put on at the school by the Gay-Straight Alliance at the school. On the front, the T-shirt said, "Be Ashamed, Our School Embraced What God Has Condemned," and on the back, it said "Homosexuality Is Shameful." The principal insisted that Harper take off the T-shirt. Harper sued, claiming this violated his First Amendment rights.

Harper's speech is constitutionally unprotected, the Ninth Circuit . . . ruled . . . in an opinion written by Judge [Stephen] Reinhardt and joined by Judge [Sidney] Thomas; Judge [Alex] Kozinski dissented. According to the majority, "derogatory and injurious remarks directed at students' minority status such as race, religion, and sexual orientation"—which essentially means expressions of viewpoints that are hostile to certain races, religions, and sexual orientations—are simply unpro-

Eugene Volokh, "Sorry, Your Viewpoint Is Excluded from First Amendment Protection," *The Volokh Conspiracy*, www.volokh.com, April 20, 2006. Reproduced by permission.

tected by the First Amendment in K–12 schools. Such speech, Judge Reinhardt said, violates "the rights of other students" by constituting a "verbal assault that may destroy the self-esteem of our most vulnerable teenagers and interfere with their educational development."

This isn't limited to, say, threats, or even personalized insults aimed at individual students. Nor is there even a "severe or pervasive" requirement such as that requirement to make speech into "hostile environment harassment" (a theory that poses its own constitutional problems, but at least doesn't restrict individual statements).

Rather, any T-shirt that condemns homosexuality is apparently unprotected. So are "display[s of the] Confederate Flag," and T-shirts that say "All Muslims Are Evil Doers."

So presumably would be T-shirts that depict some of the Mohammed cartoons [a controversial set of allegedly anti-Islamic editorial cartoons published in a Danish newspaper in 2005], as the dissent quite plausibly suggests—note that the majority's Confederate flag example makes clear that even ambiguous statements are stripped of protection if they can be seen as insulting based on race, religion, or sexual orientation. So perhaps might be T-shirts that condemn illegal aliens, since those too are directed at "minority status such as race, religion, and sexual orientation" (the "such as" makes clear that race, religion, and sexual orientation needn't be the only "minority status[es]" that would get special protection from offensive viewpoints).

The majority "reaffirm[s] the importance of preserving student speech about controversial issues generally." But, according to the constitution, this First Amendment principle somehow omits speech about controversial issues having to do with race, religion, or sexual orientation.

The Gay-Straight Alliance has a constitutional right to argue that homosexuality is quite proper, that same-sex marriages should be recognized, that discrimination based on sexual orientation should be banned, and that antigay bigotry is an abomination. But when the other side of this debate "about controversial issues" wants to express its views, which will often have to rest on the theory that homosexuality is wrong, sorry, apparently it's not important to preserve student speech that expresses that view.

"[T]here is an equality of status in the field of ideas," the Supreme Court has said. "Under the First Amendment there is no such thing as a false idea." "The government must abstain from regulating speech when the specific motivating ideology or the opinion or perspective of the speaker is the rationale for the restriction." And yet according to Judge Reinhardt, the First Amendment itself discriminates against viewpoints that express hostility to minority races, religions, and sexual orientations.

[The Harper ruling is] an opening to a First Amendment limited by rights to be free from offensive viewpoints.

Tinker v. Des Moines Independent School District

The Supreme Court has indeed recognized that speech in K–12 public schools must be somewhat more restrictable than speech on the street. *Tinker v. Des Moines Independent School District* (1969) made clear that student speech might be restricted when it's likely to substantially disrupt the educational process. And sometimes speech that's hostile based on race, religion, or sexual orientation—as well as speech that offends people for a wide variety of other reasons—might indeed lead to substantial disruption.

But this is at least a facially viewpoint-neutral standard that potentially applies to speech on all perspectives, and doesn't categorically cast out certain student viewpoints from

First Amendment protection. While the standard isn't without its problems, it is at least basically consistent with the First Amendment principle of "equality of status in the field of ideas."

Yet the majority specifically refrains from relying on this principle (and Judge Kozinski's dissent points out that on the facts of this case, there wasn't enough of a showing that the speech would likely cause disruption). Instead, Judge Reinhardt takes some unelaborated remarks by the Supreme Court about the First Amendment's not protecting student speech that "intrudes upon . . . the rights of other students," and fashions from them a constitutionally recognized right to be free from certain kinds of offensive viewpoints (not a right that is itself directly legally enforceable, but a right that the school may choose to assert as a justification for its viewpoint-based speech restrictions).

This is a very bad ruling, I think. It's a dangerous retreat from our tradition that the First Amendment is viewpoint-neutral. It's an opening to a First Amendment limited by rights to be free from offensive viewpoints. It's a tool for suppression of one side of public debates (about same-sex marriage, about Islam, quite likely about illegal immigration, and more) while the other side remains constitutionally protected and even encouraged by the government.

Maybe the government needs more flexibility in controlling student speech than *Tinker* provides. At the close of Judge Kozinski's opinion, he suggests that "perhaps school authorities should have greater latitude to control student speech than allowed them by [U.S. Supreme Court] Justice [Abe] Fortas's Vietnam-era opinion in *Tinker*. Perhaps Justice [Hugo] Black's concerns, expressed in his *Tinker* dissent, should have been given more weight. . . . Perhaps the narrow exceptions of *Tinker* should be broadened and multiplied. Perhaps *Tinker* should be overruled." But even if this is so, whatever rule is adopted should be a rule that the First Amendment applies—or doesn't apply—to all viewpoints equally, not that views that the court system finds "derogatory and injurious" are specially stripped of constitutional protection.

Universities Should Not Institute Speech Codes

Greg Lukianoff

Greg Lukianoff is the president of the Foundation for Individual Rights in Education.

[Since 1999] FIRE [The Foundation for Individual Rights in Education] has been fighting for free speech and academic freedom on college and university campuses across the nation, following through on the analysis and recommendations contained in a book written by FIRE's co-founders, Alan Charles Kors and Harvey A. Silvergate—*The Shadow University: The Betrayal of Liberty on America's Campuses.* Prior to working for FIRE, I was unaware of how common serious violations of students' basic free speech rights are on today's campuses. Since working at FIRE, however, I have witnessed hundreds of cases in which private and public universities have demonstrated a distressing disregard for free speech. FIRE has come to the defense of anti-war protesters, pro-war demonstrators, satirists, political activists from across the political spectrum, student newspapers, and students and faculty who often have done little more than criticize an administration or its policies, or who have tried constructively and peaceably to address pressing social or political concerns.

While violations of basic expressive rights are always troubling, it is especially disturbing when they take place at our colleges and universities—institutions that depend on an open exchange of ideas in order to fulfill their most basic mission. Colleges and universities should be the institutions where individuals enjoy the greatest possible free speech rights. Sadly, students and faculty too often have to fight for the right to

Greg Lukianoff, *Is Intellectual Diversity an Endangered Species on America's College Campuses?* Philadelphia: Committee on Health, Education, Labor, and Pensions, United States Senate, One Hundred Eighth Congress, First Session, 2003. Reproduced by permission.

express opinions that citizens outside of academia would simply take for granted as enjoying full legal protection.

Speech Codes

Despite the protections of the First Amendment at public universities and the powerful statements of commitment to free speech and academic freedom at most private liberal arts colleges and universities, many campuses still promulgate speech codes. You may wonder what we mean by "speech codes." FIRE defines a speech code as any campus regulation that punishes, forbids, heavily regulates, or restricts a substantial amount of expression that would be protected in the larger society. Our definition is straightforward and applies to all university policies whether they call themselves "speech codes" or not. In contrast to the way that such codes were put into effect during their heyday in the late 80s and early 90s, colleges today are loath to label their policies "speech codes" even when they restrict or forbid clearly protected speech. This may be a result of a series of court cases in which university speech codes were struck down as unconstitutional, or perhaps it is a reaction to public relations disasters that were generated by early attempts to regulate student speech.

But make no mistake . . . speech codes are alive and well on college campuses.

It has long been settled in constitutional law that free speech is not limited only to the pleasant or the pious.

The current generation of speech codes come in many shapes and sizes, including but not limited to e-mail policies that ban "derogatory comments," highly restrictive "free speech zone" policies, "diversity statements" with provisions that outlaw "intolerant expression," and so-called "harassment policies" that extend to speech that may "insult" or "demean."

While they may not call themselves "speech codes" anymore, a speech code by any other name still suppresses speech.

FIRE has been combating speech codes as a part of its general operations [since 1999]. We have come to the defense of thousands of individuals who have been the victims of rules and regulations that should have no place on our campuses. Drawing from that experience, we decided to undertake a colossal program that seeks to catalog the restrictive speech policies on every college and university campus across the country. The preliminary results of this massive research undertaking can be found on a public website, speechcodes.org. The website . . . features nearly 200 public and private colleges and universities. FIRE has rated each of the non-sectarian universities using a "lighting scheme": green lights indicate that we found no policy that seriously imperils speech; yellow lights indicate that a university has some policies that could ban or excessively regulate protected speech; and red lights are awarded to universities that have policies that ban a substantial amount of what would be clearly protected speech in the larger society. Of 176 rated universities only 20 have earned green lights, while 80 earned yellows. A distressing 76—forty-three percent of the institutions rated—earned red lights.

Types of Banned Speech

Some of these red light policies are truly bizarre. For instance, Hampshire College in Massachusetts bans "psychological intimidation, and harassment of any person or pet." Others are almost quaint, like Kansas State University, which bans the use of "profane or vulgar language" when it is used in a "disruptive manner." It has long been settled in constitutional law that free speech is not limited only to the pleasant or the pious.

Some codes are remarkably broad and vague, like that of Bard College in New York, which states, "It is impermissible to engage in conduct that deliberately causes embarrassment, discomfort, or injury to other individuals or to the community as a whole." By banning speech that "discomforts," Bard takes a position that has been adopted by many colleges and universities: valuing and promoting peace and quiet at the expense of robust debate and intellectual engagement. To be sure, politeness is a commendable value, but it simply does not compare in importance to unfettered debate and discussion in a pluralistic democracy. Furthermore, it is not the place of college administrators to force students to speak in any particular fashion. Civility should, perhaps, be inculcated when a student is young, by his or her elementary school teachers and by parents. In college, it should be learned by example. Furthermore, conditioning speech on civility virtually denies the existence of justified moral outrage.

Other codes define the "protected class" of the speech code so broadly as to ban even the most basic forms of free speech. The University of California–Santa Cruz, for example, warns against speech that shows "disrespect" or "maligns" on the basis of, among other categories, "creed," "physical ability," "political views," "religion," and "socio-economic status or other differences." One can only imagine what dreary places colleges would be if students weren't even allowed to express passionate political criticisms.

Still others dangerously trivialize society's most serious crimes in an effort to get at "offensive speech." Ohio University's "Statement on Sexual Assault," for example, declares that "Sexual assault occurs along a continuum of intrusion and violation ranging from unwanted sexual comments to forced sexual intercourse." One should be very concerned about any university that cannot make a principled distinction between loutish comments and rape.

Most colleges, however, rely on this strategy: they redefine existing serious offenses to include protected expression. Hood College in Maryland, for example, defines "harassment" as "any intentionally disrespectful behavior toward others." While "disrespectful behavior" may be rude, it certainly does not rise to the level of the crime of harassment. No one denies that a college can and should ban true harassment, but hiding a speech code inside of a "racial-harassment code," for example, does not thereby magically shield a college or university from the obligations of free speech and academic freedom.

A particularly pernicious brand of speech code goes beyond punishing what one says and extends to what one feels, thinks, or believes. Transylvania University in Kentucky bans "oral, and written actions that are intellectually . . . inappropriate" if they touch upon a broad list of protected classes. Florida State University's "General Statement of Philosophy on Student Conduct and Discipline" states, "Since behavior which is not in keeping with standards acceptable to the University community is often symptomatic of attitudes, misconceptions, and emotional crises, the treatment of these attitudes, misconceptions, and emotional crises through re-education and rehabilitative activities is an essential element of the disciplinary process." All citizens should be very concerned when state universities, which often offer only a bare minimum of due process, take upon themselves the "re-education" of adult students and empower themselves to compel correct "attitudes." That is not worthy of a free nation.

Speech Zones

Another kind of speech code is the so-called "speech zone" policy, which limits protests, debates, and even pamphleteering to tiny corners of campus. FIRE has identified or fought these policies at over two dozen public universities. Until [the summer of 2003], Western Illinois University provided students with only one "Free Speech Area." This area was only available during business hours and had to be reserved five days in advance. Even within the "Free Speech Area," additional speech restrictions applied. Until FIRE intervened, Texas Tech University—a school with 28,000 students—provided only one 20-foot-wide gazebo to be used as a "Free Speech Area." Protests, demonstrations, pamphleteering, speeches, and even the distribution of newspapers had to receive prior, official approval if they were to occur outside of the "free speech" gazebo, and requests had to "be submitted at least six university working days before the intended use."

Texas Tech has since expanded the number of speech zones on campus, but FIRE continues to fight, along with a broad coalition that includes the Alliance Defense Fund, in the courts, and [with] a new student group called Students for Free Speech on the ground. We are determined to make Texas Tech grant its students the full freedoms that students at an institution of higher learning deserve—not just the bare legal minimum.

Free speech is not, nor should it ever be, a partisan issue.

Censorship Can Affect Anyone

Lest anyone think that these speech codes might not be such a threat if they are applied judiciously and fairly, they need only consult our website at www.thefire.org. . . . We have seen dozens of examples of blatant violations of the free speech rights of students and faculty members. At Harvard Business School, an editor was threatened with discipline for publishing a mildly critical political cartoon. We continue to work on behalf of a professor who was fired for "faithlessness and disloyalty" for daring to criticize the policies of the president of Shaw University in North Carolina. At California Polytechnic State University we came to the assistance of a student who had been subjected to a seven-hour hearing and found guilty of disruption for posting an "offensive" flier advertising an upcoming speech by a black conservative. The flier only contained information about the speech, the name of the speaker's book, and a photo of the speaker. FIRE is currently helping a fifty-five-year-old grandmother who is a student at SUNY

[State University of New York] Suffolk and has been found guilty of "harassment" and "intimidation" for using a single profanity in an e-mail accidentally sent to a professor. At Roger Williams University in Rhode Island . . . administrators froze an entire year's worth of printing funds for a student newspaper, *The Hawk's Right Eye*, when it published a number of controversial articles. . . .

Free speech is not, nor should it ever be, a partisan issue. Part of the brilliance of our form of government is that it binds the right of each individual to the rights of all citizens. As a society, we only enjoy the rights that the least of us receive. Therefore, all of our rights depend on the protection of even the most controversial or "politically incorrect" of us— and, rest assured, the definition of "political correctness" changes dramatically over time. However, since colleges and universities recognize that if they were really to ban all speech that offends anyone, all colleges and universities would be reduced to silence, they often apply their speech restrictions with an unconcealed double standard.

While it has been FIRE's experience that students and professors with orthodox religious views, conservative advocates, and bold satirists are more likely than others to be censored under the current campus climate, we all have a common interest in the free speech of our nation's students. While it may be the more conservative students who today feel the brunt of speech codes on campuses, it was only a generation or two ago when the shoe was on the other foot and liberal students bore that burden. The problem is censorship, pure and simple. The group that bears the brunt of censorship at any given moment in history is of academic interest, but the existence of censorship that can silence you one year and your opponent the next is the ongoing problem. Not only are all students affected by these overbroad policies—and students of every political stripe are punished if they cross certain, often arbitrary, lines—but everyone suffers when any side of an important debate is stifled, silenced, or otherwise quashed.

And make no mistake about it, the war for free speech is often not ideological at all. Campus censorship is quite often a simple, naked exercise of power. For example, at Hampton University in Virginia, the entire press run of [one issue of the] *Hampton Script* was confiscated by administrators who were angry about the paper's refusal to run a letter from the university's acting president on the front page. College and university administrators too often view criticisms of their policies as tantamount to sedition. Furthermore, many administrators censor viewpoints not to achieve an ideological purpose or ideological homogeneity, but rather to avoid having offended students conduct noisy demonstrations that embarrass the administration. But this kind of "trouble"—loud, vociferous, and often unruly dissent—is indispensable to higher education; it is not an embarrassment or an inconvenience that needs to be stamped out. American freedom may occasionally be more troublesome than the order that exists in a police state, but it is our most precious birthright.

When students and faculty do not have to fear punishment for expressing their deeply held beliefs—no matter how outrageous or unpopular—greater intellectual diversity will result.

If there is one constant in the history of free speech, it is that the censored of one generation often become the censors of the next. This vicious cycle of censorship teaches citizens to take advantage of any opportunity that they have to silence those on the other side. Students educated in this environment can hardly be blamed if they come to view speech as little more than a tool that they must do their best to deny their enemies, rather than as a sacred value. That is a terrible threat to American liberty.

FIRE hopes that we can put an end to this vicious cycle of censorship with this generation. With the help of a coalition of individuals and organizations from across the political spectrum, we can teach the current generation that a free society's cure to "bad" speech is more speech.

Legislative Remedies

It is important to mention, however, that there are grave dangers that you must avoid in congressional involvement to return free speech to campus or through any other attempt to legislate an expansion of intellectual diversity. Well-intentioned legislation designed to protect the interests of different groups of students is all too often used as an excuse for censorship. For example, the sexual harassment regulations issued by the Office for Civil Rights of the Department of Education (OCR) have been abused and misinterpreted so commonly to justify regulations that punished merely "offensive" speech that the OCR decided it needed to issue a letter of clarification [in the summer of 2003]. This letter of clarification stated what one might think would be a self-evident point: no federal regulation may be used as a justification for denying students or faculty the free speech rights that are protected under the First Amendment. The OCR incident is only the most recent example of how regulations that were passed with the best of intentions can be turned into weapons of censorship.

History shows that efforts to control either speech or the content of speech almost always result in abuse, leading to the suppression of unpopular ideas or opinions. Any bill that would ban "indoctrination" on campus, for example, or that would promise "unbiased teaching," could too easily result in a nightmare of abuse and suppression as different sides fight to label the other sides' arguments as "indoctrination" and their own as simply "truth." The best way for Congress to ensure intellectual diversity on campus is simply to work to remove the often unlawful restrictions on speech that currently exist. When students and faculty do not have to fear punishment for expressing their deeply held beliefs—no matter how outrageous or unpopular—greater intellectual diversity will result.

It would truly be a terrible thing to have a whole generation of students so unfamiliar with their basic liberties that they would not even know if they lost them.

Yet any such legislation should be crafted with great care so as to avoid undue governmental control of or influence over institutions of higher learning, particularly at private institutions. Legislation should remind public universities that they have not only a moral, but also a legal duty to protect rather than infringe upon free speech, and that speech restrictions that would be unconstitutional in the outside world are likewise unconstitutional on public university campuses, regardless of whether or not administrators believe that such restrictions would advance other values. Legislation affecting private colleges should avoid imposing the same obligations that are imposed on public campuses, since true diversity requires that private institutions be allowed to deviate and vary from the norm. What would be most helpful would be legislation that simply required private institutions to fulfill whatever promises they make in their catalogues and literature. Thus, if a private college promises intellectual diversity and academic freedom, it should be required to deliver it. FIRE is in favor of true disclosure and of private institutions living up to their promises and assurances, rather than of governmental efforts to dictate the values to which such institutions should be dedicated. If ABC College says that it is a liberal arts institution devoted to academic freedom, then it should deliver this or else be held accountable for breaking its contractual assurances to its students. Fraudulent inducement is not a part of academic freedom.

While any remedial action should be considered carefully and thoroughly, the cost of leaving things as they are is too high. One chilling example of how poorly free speech is understood and how little it is respected in higher education today is the phenomenon of newspaper thefts. For over a decade in at least five dozen documented instances, students have stolen and destroyed tens of thousands of copies of student-run newspapers on colleges and universities across the country in an effort to silence viewpoints with which they disagree. In some cases these newspapers were thrown out, and—in at least a half dozen cases—they were burned. I hope I do not need to remind you of the fate of societies of the previous century when they began burning books. In fact, this form of mob censorship has become so commonplace that [in October 2003] the Berkeley [California] City Council passed an ordinance making newspaper theft illegal. This was in part a response to an incident involving Berkeley's current mayor, Tom Bates, who stole 1,000 copies of a student newspaper after it endorsed his opponent in the mayoral race. With those in power teaching the current generation these kinds of lessons about free speech, how can we expect them to defend their own basic rights when they are threatened? It would truly be a terrible thing to have a whole generation of students so unfamiliar with their basic liberties that they would not even know if they lost them.

Universities Should Encourage Open Debate

Judith Rodin

Judith Rodin was formerly president of the University of Pennsylvania and is currently president of The Rockefeller Foundation.

A statement calling for "intimidation-free campuses," signed by a number of current and former college leaders and published in an advertisement in the *New York Times* [in October 2002] is a powerful denunciation of intimidation and intolerance aimed at Jewish and Zionist students—a denunciation with which I strongly agree.

However, I and many other presidents declined to endorse this statement, which has been circulating for some months in the academic community. Why didn't I sign? And what does that say about my support for academic freedom, and freedom from harassment, on our campuses?

As has been reported, many of us who refused to add our names to the effort, organized in part by the American Jewish Committee, did so because we felt the statement—while paying lip service to condemning intimidation "against any person, group or cause"—was seriously unbalanced. Despite requests from several presidents, the authors of the statement refused to broaden its language to recognize that Arab and Muslim students on our campuses have been subjected to at least as much harassment and intimidation as Jewish students.

Although I am personally sympathetic to the substance of the statement, my overriding responsibility as the University of Pennsylvania's president is to protect all our students from intimidation and threats of violence. Even if the letter had been more balanced, however, I might still not have signed it. I believe the best way to deal with intolerance is not through presidential statements but, rather, to expose the haters and intimidators to the public scrutiny of their peers.

Disagreement Is Not Always Comfortable

[The recent past] has seen a noticeable increase in intemperate, uncivil, and sometimes threatening or even violent exchanges on America's campuses, among pro-Palestinian, pro-Israel, Jewish, Arab, Muslim, and other groups in the aftermath of 9/11, and over recent events in the Middle East and the looming threat of a war with Iraq. People from both within and outside the academy, and on all sides of these questions, are organizing to advance their political viewpoints, to thwart what they see as threats of intimidation and bias, and to encourage colleges and their leaders to add their moral authority and financial influence to the debates.

There is nothing wrong with that. Quite the contrary: Engagement with such issues is a moral and civic responsibility shared by every faculty member, student, and college president—indeed, every American.

Inevitably, one's position on these questions is influenced by personal identities, beliefs, and political perspectives. But it is crucial to recognize that, at one point or another, and to varying degrees on many campuses, every party to these debates has felt threatened, angry, fearful, or intimidated. They all share a sense of moral rectitude and righteous self-justification. That is what makes the issues so difficult: Each side feels both threatened and justified.

It is morally and educationally essential for colleges to oppose hatred and intimidation. Likewise safety and security are prerequisites of academic life—and colleges should, and do, go to great lengths to protect our students from harm. But that is not the same as assuring that they always feel comfortable. As we learned during the era of campus speech codes, the fastest way to empower and embolden hatred and intimidation is to try to suppress it. Learning how to bring hatred and intolerance into the light of day and to engage its emotions, arguments, and rhetoric with reason and evidence may involve confrontation and discomfort, but it inevitably strengthens our students and institutions for the responsibilities of citizenship and civic engagement. Invariably, hateful ideas will crumble under the weight of relentless scrutiny and informed debate.

We cannot use the power of the presidency to try to ban hate; we must empower our students with the knowledge, self-confidence, and critical-thinking skills they need to defeat hate.

Political Debate on Campus

I have tried to emphasize the effectiveness of that approach on the Penn campus over the past eight years—whether those who felt threatened were African-Americans, Haitians, Jews, Latinos, Muslims, conservatives, or liberals.

For example, [in spring 2002], a graduate teaching assistant posted on an Internet newsgroup some extremely hateful remarks about Palestinian and Muslim people. Some outraged students and faculty members called on the administration to condemn and sanction the student. I argued, however, that even if we were willing to take such punitive measures, those actions would still leave the hateful ideas themselves unchallenged.

Instead, we sponsored a series of debates and scholarly presentations on the Middle East conflict. We promoted a constructive interfaith dialogue and conducted problem-solving group exercises among Christian, Jewish, and Muslim students. We also offered counseling support. In addition, to allay any safety concerns and protect any student group that felt especially vulnerable or threatened, we maintained a visible campus police presence. In the free exchange that ensued, the hateful comments were thoroughly dissected and discredited, and the fabric of our interfaith community grew stronger.

That has been our approach—and will continue to be—with other similar situations. We certainly do not remain aloof from the pain felt by those who are the targets of threats or hate speech, or from their deeply felt concerns for their own safety. But we don't respond to intimidation with more intimidation.

Others may do as their own sense of professional responsibility dictates, but I will stay the course of encouraging, rather than discouraging, the most robust and engaged debate possible—even, and especially, with those who would seek to intimidate or threaten their opponents. Public confrontation is their greatest enemy, not presidential statements. The only way to have an "intimidation-free" campus is to not let ourselves be intimidated.

School Libraries Should Not Restrict Access to Any Books

Chris Crutcher

Chris Crutcher is the author of several award-winning novels for young adults, including Whale Talk, Running Loose, *and* Staying Fat for Sarah Byrnes.

To the Students of the Limestone School District:

Recently my book, *Whale Talk*, was banned in your school district, and I thought I might address that. First, let it be known that I don't take it personally. None of the four school board members who voted to take the book out of your reach knows me and I have no reason to believe any of them bear me ill will. From all I have read, I believe the stated reason the book was banned was for "curses", which, where I come from are called "cuss words."

Arguably the two most offensive passages in the story occur when a four and a half year old bi-racial girl screams out the names she is called on a regular basis by her racist stepfather and later when that same racist stepfather is drunkenly threatening the foster family that is keeping her safe.

In the 1980's and early 1990's when I was working as a child abuse and neglect therapist in the Spokane (Washington) Community Mental Health Center, I worked with a young bi-racial girl living in circumstances much like those depicted in the book. Her biological father didn't even know of her existence and her mother didn't have the emotional strength to keep her out of the eye of the hurricane of her stepfather's hatred. She couldn't eat at the table until her younger, white stepbrothers had finished. She wasn't allowed to play with toys

Chris Crutcher, "To the Students of the Limestone School Disctrict," Chris Crutcher's Authorized Web Site, March 2005. Reproduced by permission.

until they were broken and handed over to her. The first time I saw her she was standing over a sink, trying to wash the brown off her skin so her (step) daddy would love her. Time and time again in therapy she expressed the self-contempt she had gained believing there was something fundamentally wrong with her because there was no way to find acceptance in her world. In play therapy she was allowed to work through her life trauma to ultimately better understand that it was not her fault she was treated as she was, and to come to a better understanding (in a four-year-old's way of understanding) of the world she lived in. The language that little girl used was even tougher than what my character used in *Whale Talk*.

When *Whale Talk* gets challenged or banned, it's often because a parent who hasn't read the book runs across that passage or one like it, sees the words (which in this case are in large font because the little girl is screaming) and decides they are a danger to you. They describe the story, more often than not without reading it, as obscene or vulgar or evil—or all three.

I think it obscene that [a] school board doesn't trust [adolescents] enough to know that [they] can read harsh stories, told in their native tongue, and make decisions for [themselves].

Life Is More Obscene than Fiction

But what's truly obscene is that I know a real girl in the real world who has gone through this. What's obscene is that so do you, even if you're not aware of the specifics. What's obscene is that you know kids who have gone through, and are going through, worse.

What's obscene is that kids who are mal-treated often grow up angry and depressed and anxious and desperate. They experience crippling difficulties in school, in social relations and in all matters of self-esteem. They use the language I use in the story and worse because it is all they have to try to match what is inside to the outside world. They need to be recognized, and brought into your fold. Often we adults can't help them, but you can. I write the stories I write to bring things like this to your attention because I believe if kids who are treated badly are to survive, they will survive through the acceptance of their peers, and that acceptance will come from understanding. It's true; I'm asking a lot from you.

Let me tell you something else I think is obscene. I think it obscene that your school board doesn't trust you enough to know you can read harsh stories, told in their native tongue, and make decisions for yourself what you think of the issues or the language. It is astonishing to me that grown men, in this case, don't believe you can think for yourselves. Some of you could have voted in the last election. Many more of you will be eligible in the next. Some of you may be going to war.

Students' Intellectual Freedom

It is not a big deal that *Whale Talk* was removed from your school library shelves. There are plenty of good books out there that your school board hasn't had a chance to ban yet. But consider this.

I . . . encourage [adolescents] to stand up for [their] own intellectual freedom; to choose what [they] want to read about and talk about and explore.

About a decade ago, a stellar author named Walter Dean Myers wrote *Fallen Angels*, a story about a young African American man fighting in Vietnam. Walter told his story, using the language of soldiers at war. It was pretty much the language I used to talk about this four-year-old girl, who was also at war. *Fallen Angels*, a critically acclaimed book, is constantly under the same attack that *Whale Talk* is under from

131

your school board. Think about this a minute. In the not too distant future many of you will be soldiers also asked to fight in the name of your country. Statistics say a few of your number will also be writers. Imagine risking your life in war, coming back to tell your story in as real a fashion as you can, only to have your children told they can't read your story in your school because the school board won't tolerate the realistic language in which you tell it. They not only tell their children it can't be part of their education, they tell your children it can't be part of their education.

I have no problem at all with any or all of you picking up *Whale Talk*, reading a couple of chapters, or even a couple of pages, not liking it, slamming it shut and never opening it again. I don't even have a problem with that if you do it because you are offended by the situations—or the language. I don't have a problem with that because it's your choice. I trust you to know what you like and what you don't, and what's good for you in terms of literature; the same way the United States Supreme Court trusted high school students when they ruled in their favor in the landmark case known as the *Board of Education vs. Pico*.

I can't change the minds of people who believe that the best way to keep kids safe is to keep you ignorant. What I can, and will, do is this: Donate copies of *Whale Talk* to your public library, which is a lot less likely to try to think for you. I can urge you to take a look at it and decide for yourselves. I can encourage you to stand up for your own intellectual freedom; to choose what you want to read about and talk about and explore. I can encourage you to let those members of your school board who don't trust you with tough material, know you are a lot more savvy than they think you are, and that there is no way they can capture your intellectual freedom with the silliness of banning a book from the library shelves. There are plenty of places to get books.

Good Literature Examines Tough Issues

I have to be honest. I don't think the only reason those four school board members wanted *Whale Talk* out of your schools was language. I could be wrong—it's certainly happened before—but I think there are other issues in the book that make them uncomfortable. But even on language alone, if you accept the banning of this book, you should demand that they also remove other books in which that language exists. Start with Alice Walker's Pulitzer Prize–winning *The Color Purple*, then go to Maya Angelou's *I Know Why the Caged Bird Sings*. You certainly can't allow any of my other ten books there, nor any of Robert Cormiers, many of Walter Dean Myers' or Tim O'Brien's (*The Things They Carried* may well be one of the ten best written books of the twentieth century). Sherman Alexi, the great Native American writer, is out, hands down and there is no way you can be allowed to cast your eyes upon Joseph Heller's *Catch-22*. If you accept this "protection" from your school board, demand that they step up and truly protect you.

I may seem somewhat flip here but I believe that adolescence is an extremely important time in any human's development. There are hundreds of questions about relationships and career and identity, and you are handcuffed to look at them when a group of men who believe that the depiction of true, rough language is a top-priority moral issue. I trust you to read my book, or any of the other, far more familiar books mentioned above, and decide for yourselves what you think of them. It wouldn't be completely over the top for you to expect your school board to do the same. Remember this: your school board is there to make decisions to further your education, not keep themselves in their own comfort zones.

I do want to compliment those members and the superintendent who voted against the banning. It does my heart good to know there are many educators out there who understand

that good education requires the opening rather than the clos-
ing of minds. Again, this isn't about *Whale Talk*, it really isn't.
It's about you.

Sincerely,

Chris Crutcher

High Schools and Universities Should Not Censor Student Newspapers

Mike Hiestand

Mike Hiestand is a legal consultant for the Student Press Law Center, an organization that advocates students' free-press rights.

> "We need not now decide whether the same degree of deference [to censorship by school officials] is appropriate with respect to school-sponsored expressive activities at the college and university level."
>
> —*Hazelwood School District v. Kuhlmeier* (1988)
>
> "Hazelwood provides our starting point"
>
> —*Hosty v. Carter* (2005)

For about ten years now, we've had a bit of a Chicken Little Complex at the Student Press Law Center. Worried—but not wanting to push the panic button too hard. Mindful of the criticism we heard from those charging that we were over-reacting.

Well, it turns out that Chicken Little was right: on June 20 [2005] the sky did, in fact, fall for some college student media. On that date, 11 judges sitting on the federal Seventh Circuit Court of Appeals did what none of us in the student media community obviously hoped—and I think most of us never really thought—they would do: they potentially gave college administrators in three states the same devastating censorship key handed to their high school counterparts 17 years earlier.

How did we ever reach this point? More importantly, what's next?

Mike Hiestand, *Trends in College Media*. Minneapolis, MN: Associated Collegiate Press, 2006. © Copyright 1999–2006 Associated Collegiate Press. Reproduced by permission.

The *Hazelwood* Decision

In 1988, in a 5-3 decision, the U.S. Supreme Court ruled in *Hazelwood School District v. Kuhlmeier* that public high school officials had significant authority to censor most (not all) student newspapers and other forms of student expression sponsored by the school. While the censorship power of high school administrators under *Hazelwood* was not unlimited, the decision created expansive new categories of "unprotected" speech, shocking in their vagueness and breadth. Instead of just "libel" or "obscenity," for example, high school officials, the Court said, could now censor speech if a principal deemed it "poorly written," "ungrammatical," "biased" or "inconsistent with the shared values of a civilized social order."

Read those categories again. The *Hazelwood* Court didn't merely adjust the First Amendment balance between administrative authority and student free speech rights, it pretty much tossed out the scale.

If there was any good news in the *Hazelwood* decision, it was only that the decision could have been even worse. For one thing, the Court gave college students a temporary pass. It declined to say that a public college president, for example, should have the same authority as a high school principal to censor a student's "poorly written" or "biased" editorial. The Court in 1988 said that was a question for another day.

The *Kincaid* Decision

That day didn't come for almost eight years. Our first official warning went out in November 1995 after students at Kentucky State University filed a lawsuit against university officials who had seized their student yearbook after it came back from the printer. Among the yearbook's alleged offenses, according to school administrators: its cover was purple instead of yellow and green, KSU's official colors.

As ludicrous as the reasons for the censorship were, the fact remained that state officials at a public university had locked some 2,000 copies of an otherwise completely lawful college student yearbook away in a closet and had refused to back down. More importantly, the university claimed *Hazelwood* gave them the authority to do so.

Despite some scary early rulings from both the federal district court and a 3-judge appellate panel, a full panel of judges of the U.S. Sixth Circuit Court of Appeals recognized the importance of free speech on a college campus and, in January 2001, issued a strong decision rejecting KSU's attempt to bring *Hazelwood* to public university student newsrooms.

Truly free school-sponsored speech will exist on public college campuses only so long as administrators on that campus want it to exist.

The *Hosty* Decision

Despite the ruling in *Kincaid*, later that year Illinois' Attorney General [AG] decided to take another shot—with another court—at bringing *Hazelwood* to America's college and university campuses. Student newspaper editors at Governor's State University sued school officials for halting publication of their student newspaper absent administrative prior review and approval of future issues. The state's chief lawyer argued such action was just fine, citing *Hazelwood*. This time, the students won at both the district court and before a three-judge panel of the U.S. Seventh Circuit Court. Appeals. But on June 20, seven appellate judges bought into the Illinois AG's argument and reversed the lower court rulings, officially opening the college door to *Hazelwood*. Four judges strongly dissented. In weighing the rights of college students, the court majority wrote, "Hazelwood provides our starting point."

I'm sure Abe Lincoln would be proud.

For proponents of a free press, the decision is hard to sugarcoat. It changes things. For college journalists in the three states covered by the Seventh Circuit—Illinois, Indiana and Wisconsin—the answer to the question "Can they censor?" is no longer always a clear and easy call. Most of the time—at least for now—the answer will still be "no." If school officials have recognized their student media—either by policy or practice—as "designated public forums" (yes, it gets complicated) and allow student editors to determine their own editorial content, *Hazelwood* 's lesser standards still won't apply. The Seventh Circuit made clear that in a designated public forum student newspaper, "no censorship [is] allowed."

Currently, almost every public college student newspaper in the country operates like a public forum because up until now it seemed clear that is what the law required. But for students in the Seventh Circuit, *Hosty* means that college officials may now have a choice. "Public forum" status is not automatic. And as hundreds of examples at the high school level have shown over the past several years, where a student publication is sponsored by the school, administrators can—if they do so carefully—take steps that make it unlikely a court would recognize the publication as a designated public forum.

Let there be no doubt: giving college officials such a "choice" puts student newspapers—and every other university-sponsored expressive activity—at risk. Thanks to the Seventh Circuit, the new reality may be that truly free school-sponsored speech will exist on public college campuses only so long as administrators on that campus want it to exist.

The First Amendment for the New Millennium: Congress shall make no law—unless it wants to.

Modern Civics Education

"Such unthinking contempt for individual rights is intolerable from any state official. It is particularly insidious from one to whom the public entrusts the task of inculcating in its youth an appreciation for the cherished democratic liberties that our Constitution guarantees."

—*Justice [William] Brennan's dissent,*
Hazelwood v. Kuhlmeier (1988)

The effects of *Hazelwood* on our public secondary schools have been predictable. The government officials running our high schools did exactly what the Founding Fathers knew government officials would always do absent a clear limit on their ability to control speech: they exercised such control. Administrative censorship of high school student media since 1988 has skyrocketed. Calls for legal help to the Student Press Law Center are up more than four-fold. Newspapers at many high schools have taken on the look and feel of the school district's public relations office. Others have simply folded up shop.

More troubling than any of that, however, is that students started to graduate from high school without the foggiest notion of a living First Amendment and why it is relevant and vital to how things are supposed to work in our country. The high school years are often our newest citizens' first introduction to the idea of what it means to be a participant in the United States. For many, it will be their only formal civics education before we call upon them to start taking an active role in the process of self-government. Certainly, for way too many of the students that called our office for help over the past 17 years—and for the countless others who never even bothered—this introduction to American civics has been sorry indeed.

"I'm sorry," I would often be forced to explain, "but I'm afraid the First Amendment isn't going to be of much help."

It made no difference whether they were calling about an editorial in favor of school prayer or a column defending same-sex marriages. They had, sometimes for the first time in their lives, chosen to publicly take a stand and to have their voice heard. To exercise a basic right they had been told—and they believed—belonged to all Americans.

It hurt—each and every time—to hear that bubble burst at the end of the phone line.

I sincerely hope those students will give the First Amendment another shot. Perhaps, at some point in the future, they will see how a free press really can work and how it truly is worth standing up for and defending. The way things are going, we're going to need every one of them.

More than a third of all high school students believe the First Amendment 'goes too far' in guaranteeing freedom of speech and freedom of the press.

The Road Ahead

I have a quote that hangs in my office from Horace Mann, frequently referred to as the "Father of American Education." Back in 1845 he wrote:

"The great moral attribute of self-government cannot be born and matured in a day; and if school children are not trained to it, we only prepare ourselves for disappointment if we expect it from grown men. . . . As the fitting apprenticeship for despotism consists in being trained to despotism, so the fitting apprenticeship for self-government consists in being trained to self-government."

Well, thanks in part to nearly two decades of *Hazelwood*, I can attest that the training of our high school students—and the disappointment—appears nearly complete.

College advisers routinely tell me that many of the students entering their newsrooms simply don't understand the press's role. About questioning authority. About seeking and covering the news, no matter how controversial the topic. About confirming the authenticity of statements made in a university press release prior to publication. Or instinctively challenging administrative attempts to dictate what they print. This, it was clear to their college advisers, simply wasn't done—or even discussed—in high school. They were *Hazelwood*-ized.

The recent national survey by the Knight Foundation—which, among other disturbing results, revealed that more than a third of all high school students believe the First Amendment "goes too far" in guaranteeing freedom of speech and freedom of the press—certainly conforms to the findings of the college advisers I spoke with.

Apparently not bothered by such results, however, the Illinois Attorney General and the federal judges of the Seventh Circuit Court of Appeals have now chosen to take *Hazelwood*—and its First Amendment Lite brand of civics education—to college. There is no telling whether the U.S Supreme Court, who gave us the decision in the first place, will see fit to step in now and limit—or embrace—its extension to the university setting.

"It is a sad day for journalism in the United States," Society of Professional Journalists President Irwin Gratz said, ". . . students [affected by *Hosty*] will now spend eight years with prior review and censorship as part of their journalistic experience."

It's a sad day for much more than journalism.

One must ask: How do we go from thinking of American college and university campuses as the "quintessential marketplace of ideas," as courts referred to them not so long ago, to places where state officials may now be permitted to censor student speech when they determine it is "inconsistent with the shared values of a civilized social order?"

It is a question whose answer, I think Horace Mann would agree, says much about the direction we, as a country, are headed.

CHAPTER 3

Should Pornographic and Violent Material Be Censored?

Censoring Pornographic and Violent Material: An Overview

Henry Cohen

Henry Cohen is a legislative attorney in the American Law division of the Congressional Research Service.

The First Amendment to the United States Constitution provides that "Congress shall make no law . . . abridging the freedom of speech, or of the press. . . ." This language restricts government both more and less than it would if it were applied literally. It restricts government more in that it applies not only to Congress, but to all branches of the federal government, and to all branches of state and local government. It restricts government less in that it provides no protection to some types of speech and only limited protection to others.

This report provides an overview of the major exceptions to the First Amendment—of the ways that the Supreme Court has interpreted the guarantee of freedom of speech and press to provide no protection or only limited protection for some types of speech. For example, the Court has decided that the First Amendment provides no protection to obscenity, child pornography, or speech that constitutes "advocacy of the use of force or of law violation . . . where such advocacy is directed to inciting or producing imminent lawless action and is likely to incite or produce such action."

The Court has also decided that the First Amendment provides less than full protection to commercial speech, defamation (libel and slander), speech that may be harmful to children, speech broadcast on radio and television, and public employees' speech. Even speech that enjoys the most extensive First Amendment protection may be subject to "regulations of

Henry Cohen, "Freedom of Speech and Press: Exceptions to the First Amendment," *Congressional Research Service*, May 24, 2005.

the time, place, and manner of expression which are content-neutral, are narrowly tailored to serve a significant government interest, and leave open ample alternative channels of communication." And, even speech that enjoys the most extensive First Amendment protection may be restricted on the basis of its content if the restriction passes "strict scrutiny," *i.e.*, if the government shows that the restriction serves "to promote a compelling interest" and is "the least restrictive means to further the articulated interest."

Obscenity

Obscenity apparently is unique in being the only type of speech to which the Supreme Court has denied First Amendment protection without regard to whether it is harmful to individuals. According to the Court, there is evidence that, at the time of the adoption of the First Amendment, obscenity "was outside the protection intended for speech and press." Consequently, obscenity may be banned simply because a legislature concludes that banning it protects "the social interest in order and morality." No actual harm, let alone compelling governmental interest, need be shown in order to ban it.

What is obscenity? It is not synonymous with pornography, as most pornography is not legally obscene; *i.e.*, most pornography is protected by the First Amendment. To be obscene, pornography must, at a minimum, "depict or describe patently offensive 'hard core' sexual conduct." The Supreme Court has created a three-part test, known as the *Miller* test, to determine whether a work is obscene. The *Miller* test asks:

(a) whether the "average person applying contemporary community standards" would find that the work, taken as a whole, appeals to the prurient interest; (b) whether the work depicts or describes, in a patently offensive way, sexual conduct specifically defined by the applicable state law; and (c) whether the work, taken as a whole, lacks serious literary, artistic, political, or scientific value.

The Supreme Court has clarified that only "the first and second prongs of the *Miller* test—appeal to prurient interest and patent offensiveness—are issues of fact for the jury to determine applying contemporary community standards." As for the third prong, "[t]he proper inquiry is not whether an ordinary member of any given community would find serious literary, artistic, political, or scientific value in allegedly obscene material, but whether a reasonable person would find such value in the material, taken as a whole."

The Supreme Court has allowed one exception to the rule that obscenity is not protected by the First Amendment: one has a constitutional right to possess obscene material "in the privacy of his own home." However, there is no constitutional right to provide obscene material for private use or even to acquire it for private use.

Child Pornography

Child pornography is material that visually depicts sexual conduct by children. It is unprotected by the First Amendment even when it is not obscene; *i.e.*, child pornography need not meet the *Miller* test to be banned. Because of the legislative interest in destroying the market for the exploitative use of children, there is no constitutional right to possess child pornography even in the privacy of one's own home.

Speech that is otherwise fully protected by the First Amendment may be restricted in order to protect children.

In 1996, Congress enacted the Child Pornography Protection Act (CPPA), which defined "child pornography" to include visual depictions that *appear* to be of a minor, even if no minor is actually used. The Supreme Court, however, declared the CPPA unconstitutional to the extent that it prohibited pictures that are produced without actual minors. Pornography that uses actual children may be banned because laws against it target "[t]he production of the work, not its content"; the CPPA, by contrast, targeted the content, not the production. The government "may not prohibit speech because it increases the chance an unlawful act will be committed 'at some indefinite future time.'" In 2003, Congress responded by enacting Title V of the PROTECT Act, P.L. 108-21, which prohibits any "digital image, computer image, or computer-generated image that is, or is indistinguishable from, that of a minor engaging in sexually explicit conduct." It also prohibits "a visual depiction of any kind, including a drawing, cartoon, sculpture, or painting, that . . . depicts a minor engaging in sexually explicit conduct," and is obscene or lacks serious literary, artistic, political, or scientific value. . . .

Speech Harmful to Children

Speech that is otherwise fully protected by the First Amendment may be restricted in order to protect children. This is because the Court has "recognized that there is a compelling interest in protecting the physical and psychological well-being of minors." However, any restriction must be accomplished "'by narrowly drawn regulations without unnecessarily interfering with First Amendment freedoms.' It is not enough to show that the government's ends are compelling; the means must be carefully tailored to achieve those ends."

Thus, the government may prohibit the sale to minors of material that it deems "harmful to minors" ("so called 'girlie' magazines"), whether or not they are not obscene to adults. It may prohibit the broadcast of "indecent" language on radio and television during hours when children are likely to be in the audience, but it may not ban it around the clock unless it is obscene. Federal law currently bans indecent broadcasts between 6 a.m. and 10 p.m. Similarly, Congress may not ban dial-a-porn, but it may (as it does at 47 U.S.C. § 223) prohibit it from being made available to minors or to persons who have not previously requested it in writing.

In *Reno v. American Civil Liberties Union*, the Supreme Court declared unconstitutional two provisions of the Communications Decency Act (CDA) that prohibited indecent communications to minors on the Internet. The Court held that the CDA's "burden on adult speech is unacceptable if less restrictive alternatives would be at least as effective in achieving the legitimate purpose that the statute was enacted to serve." "[T]he governmental interest in protecting children from harmful materials ... does not justify an unnecessarily broad suppression of speech addressed to adults. As we have explained, the Government may not 'reduc[e] the adult population ... to ... only what is fit for children.'"

The Court distinguished the Internet from radio and television because (1) "[t]he CDA's broad categorical prohibitions are not limited to particular times and are not dependent on any evaluation by an agency familiar with the unique characteristics of the Internet," (2) the CDA imposes criminal penalties, and the Court has never decided whether indecent broadcasts "would justify a criminal prosecution," and (3) radio and television, unlike the Internet, have, "as a matter of history ... 'received the most limited First Amendment protection, ... in large part because warnings could not adequately protect the listener from unexpected program content.... [On the Internet], the risk of encountering indecent material by accident is remote because a series of affirmative steps is required to access specific material."

In 1998, Congress enacted the Child Online Protection Act (COPA), P.L. 105-277, title XIV, to replace the CDA. COPA differs from the CDA in two main respects: (1) it prohibits communication to minors only of "material that is harmful to minors," rather than material that is indecent, and (2) it applies only to communications for commercial purposes on publicly accessible websites. COPA has not taken effect, because a constitutional challenge was brought, and the district court, finding a likelihood that the plaintiffs would prevail, issued a preliminary injunction against enforcement of the statute, pending a trial on the merits. The Third Circuit affirmed, but, in 2002, in *Ashcroft v. American Civil Liberties Union*, the Supreme Court held that COPA's use of community standards to define "material that is harmful to minors" does not by itself render the statute unconstitutional. The Supreme Court, however, did not remove the preliminary injunction against enforcement of the statute, and remanded the case to the Third Circuit to consider whether it is unconstitutional nonetheless. In 2003, the Third Circuit again found the plaintiffs likely to prevail and affirmed the preliminary injunction. In 2004, the Supreme Court affirmed the preliminary injunction because it found that the government had failed to show that filtering prohibited material would not be as effective in accomplishing Congress's goals. It remanded the case for trial, however, and did not foreclose the district court from concluding otherwise.

Indecent Broadcasts Should Be Censored

L. Brent Bozell III

L. Brent Bozell III is the founder and president of the Media Research Center, an organization that fights liberal bias in the media.

In the surging surf of the trashy tidal wave known as the Super Bowl Halftime Show, radio shock jocks are a very unhappy lot. Whether it's Howard Stern or Don and Mike, the airwaves today are filled with whining and complaining about the newly restrictive atmosphere emanating from the Washington offices of the Federal Communications Commission, FCC, and Congress.

The shock jocks make it sound like we've entered a Brave New World of autocratic censorship. The House has passed legislation by a resounding 391-22 margin that would, among other things, increase fines [for broadcast indecency] almost twenty-fold, to $500,000, with license-revocation hearings after three offenses. The FCC for its part has stated it intends to get very serious about curbing the abuses on the airwaves. In short, the old formula—look for the next boundary of taste to bowl over—doesn't look like such a smart play right now.

Opponents of the new trend cry repression, censorship, the repeal of the First Amendment. But is the new trend censorship—or democracy?

Voters Prefer Censorship

Ten years ago, the debate raged over offensive images of "Piss Christ" and Robert Mapplethorpe's sexualized photos of naked young children, subsidized by every American taxpayer

L. Brent Bozell III, "Censorship—Or Democracy?" *Creators Syndicate*, March 12, 2004. By permission L. Brent Bozell III and Creators Syndicate, Inc.

through the National Endowment for the Arts [NEA]. NEA lovers cried "censorship." But by funding offensive "art" without consulting the taxpayers, the real government-dictated or government-favored speech came from the NEA's cultural commissars, not the protesters. If the American people were allowed to vote on whether they would spend their pennies on "Piss Christ," the vast majority would veto that ridiculous expenditure.

When the most debased programming ... is exposed to the broad mass of the American people, they go from passively unaware to actively outraged.

Broadcast speech is not subsidized in the same way as NEA art—although the regulatory rationale for the FCC is based on the principle that the airwaves belong to the public. Radio and TV stations merely make a mint off them. The political problem for shock jocks is that when their "finest" work is held up to public scrutiny, most people can't believe they actually say and do these incredibly perverted things. They like the idea that the FCC actually upholds the broadcast-obscenity laws that have long been on the books.

The Super Bowl sleazefest taught Washington and Los Angeles that when the most debased programming narrowcasted in the neatly compartmentalized youth culture—MTV, Howard Stern, *South Park*, you name it—is exposed to the broad mass of the American people, they go from passively unaware to actively outraged. Entertainment barons only care about the wallets of the young adults who show up in the ratings counts. Activists concerned about the degradation of the broader culture have gone to Washington demanding action to protect the airwaves they—and not Viacom—own.

It's not censorship, it's democracy. It's community activism, free speech rising up to combat other free speech. Should a station be fined, and maybe even lose its license for repeated violations? Yes. If that's the only way to get the media giants to behave, so be it.

Censorship Hypocrisy

There's also a dollop of hypocrisy in the "censorship" complaints. When the offensive content is political instead of sexual—remember the infamous incident when the D.C. shock jock "The Greaseman" said black singer Lauryn Hill was so bad he could see why blacks get dragged behind trucks?—nobody warns of "censorship" or lectures about the First Amendment. They pack the shock jock's bags.

The hypocrisy doesn't end there, either. When the news media confronts the topic of broadcast indecency, they are quick to give credibility to the "censorship" argument, but then censor out the very content that's under discussion. News reports on Clear Channel sacking the Florida shock jock "Bubba the Love Sponge" after a $755,000 fine didn't often explain the kind of skits "Bubba" did.

In one skit, using cartoon music, he imagined favorite kiddie cartoon characters in sexual situations, with cartoon theme songs in the background. Shaggy was hooked on crack, so Scooby-Doo told him he could perform oral sex acts to pay for the drugs. George Jetson tells his wife Jane he doesn't need Viagra because he's got a "Spacely Sprocket (bleep) ring," which then malfunctions. Alvin the Chipmunk complains he hasn't had sex in six weeks. Another chipmunk responds that it's the "(bleep)-ing pussy music we play" and begins to sing a more "kick ass" song directing a "filthy chipmunk-whore" to perform oral sex on him.

How many parents would vote to have their children vulnerable to this garbage on the public airwaves daily? You can whine until the cows come home, Howard Stern. The public is fed up with you and your lot.

Internet Pornography Should Be Restricted

Phyllis Schlafly

Phyllis Schlafly, founder of the Eagle Forum, has been a leading pro-family conservative activist since the 1960s.

Do you ever wonder why the Internet is so polluted with pornography? The Supreme Court just reminded us why: it blocks every attempt by Congress to regulate the pornographers.

From its ivory tower, the Court props open the floodgates for smut and graphic sex. Over the past [several] years, it has repeatedly found new constitutional rights for vulgarity, most recently invalidating the Child Online Protection Act (COPA).

This latest judicial outrage happened on the final day of the Supreme Court term, after which the justices headed out for a long summer break. Lacking teenaged children of their own, the justices closed their eyes to electronic obscenity polluting our children's minds.

The Supreme Court Favors Pornographers

For decades, pornographers have enjoyed better treatment by our courts than any other industry. The justices have constitutionally protected obscenity in libraries, filth over cable television, and now unlimited Internet pornography.

The flood of pornography started with the Warren Court when it handed down 34 decisions between 1966 and 1970 in favor of the smut peddlers. In mostly one-sentence decisions that were issued anonymously (the justices were too cowardly to sign them), the Court overturned every attempt by communities to maintain standards of decency.

Phyllis Schlafly, "Supreme Court Sides with Pornographers, Again," *Eagle Forum*, July 14, 2004. Reproduced by permission.

The judges' obsession with smut is astounding. Even though five Supreme Court justices were appointed by Presidents [Ronald] Reagan and the first [George] Bush, graphic sex wins judicial protection in essentially every case.

Woe to those who transgress an obscure environmental law, or say a prayer before a football game, or run a political ad within two months of an election. They find no judicial sympathy, as courts now routinely restrict private property rights and censor political speech.

But the pornographers can do no wrong in the eyes of our top justices. The most explicit sex can be piped into our home computers and the Supreme Court prevents our democratically elected officials from doing anything about it.

The Supreme Court insisted that individual Internet users should buy filters to try to block the vulgarity. Should those who do not like air pollution be told to buy air masks?

The Child Online Protection Act

COPA was enacted by Congress in response to the Court's invalidation of the predecessor law, the Communications Decency Act of 1996. But decency lost again when six justices knocked out COPA in *Ashcroft v. ACLU*.

COPA was badly needed, as filth plagues the Internet, incites sex crimes, and entraps children. COPA banned the posting for "commercial purposes" on the World Wide Web of material that is "patently offensive" in a sexual manner unless the poster takes reasonable steps to restrict access by minors.

You don't need to look very far to find a tragic crime traceable to the Internet. In New Jersey in 1997, 15-year-old Sam Manzie, who had fallen prey to homosexual conduct prompted by the Internet, sexually assaulted and murdered 11-year-old Eddie Werner, who was selling candy door-to-door.

COPA did not censor a single word or picture. Instead, it merely required the purveyors of sex-for-profit to screen their websites from minors, which can be done by credit card or other verification.

But minors are an intended audience for the highly profitable sex industry. Impressionable teenagers are most easily persuaded to have abortions, and homosexual clubs in high school are designed for the young.

Justice [Anthony] Kennedy declared it unconstitutional for Congress to stop porn flowing to teens, shifting the burden to families to screen out the graphic sex rather than imposing the cost on the companies profiting from the filth. His reasoning is as absurd as telling a family just to pull down its window shades if it doesn't want to see people exposing themselves outside.

In a prior pro-porn decision, Kennedy cited Hollywood morals as a guide for America, but this time he relied on the prevalence of foreign pornography. "40% of harmful-to-minors content comes from overseas," he declared in holding that the other 60% of obscenity is wrapped in the First Amendment.

The Supreme Court insisted that individual Internet users should buy filters to try to block the vulgarity. Should those who do not like air pollution be told to buy air masks?

The Supreme Court protects pornography in books, movies, cable television, and the Internet, real or simulated, against all citizens' clean-up efforts. The Court is no longer the blindfolded lady weighing a controversy, but is dominated by media-driven supremacists forcing us down into a moral sewer.

This latest pro-porn decision was too much even for [President Bill] Clinton-appointed Justice [Stephen] Breyer. He said, "Congress passed the current statute in response to the Court's decision" invalidating the prior law; "what else was Congress supposed to do?"

The solution to these ills foisted on us by judicial supremacists is for Congress to exercise its constitutional powers to remove jurisdiction from the federal courts over pornography. The Court has abused its power, and it's Congress's duty to end the judicial abuse.

Virtual Child Pornography Should Be Banned

Ernest E. Allen

Ernest E. Allen is the president and chief executive officer of the National Center for Missing and Exploited Children.

Mr. Chairman and members of the [U.S. House of Representatives Judiciary] Committee, I am pleased to appear before your Subcommittee [on crime] today and express my views and those of the National Center for Missing & Exploited Children (NCMEC) regarding the probable impact of the Supreme Court's recent decision in the case of *Ashcroft v. the Free Speech Coalition* [which declared that virtual child pornography that does not depict an actual child is protected speech under the First Amendment]. Our views are very basic and straightforward:

1. We believe that the Court's decision will result in the proliferation of child pornography in America, unlike anything we have seen in more than twenty years;

2. We believe that due to advances in imaging technology, actual child pornography and virtual child pornography have become virtually indistinguishable; and

3. We believe that as a result of the Court's decision, thousands of children will be sexually victimized, most of whom will not report the offense. . . .

Efforts to Fight Child Pornography

While we are perhaps best known for our work in the field of missing children, NCMEC is also a leader in the battle against child sexual exploitation and has become the epicenter of the war against child pornography. How did we become such a central figure in the child pornography battle?

Ernest E. Allen, "Testimony to the U.S. House of Representatives Judiciary Committee, Subcommittee on Crime," May 1, 2002. Reproduced by permission.

- The Child Porn Tipline was launched in June 1987 as a service for the U.S. Customs Service and subsequently for the U.S. Postal Inspection Service [U.S.P.I.S.]. In partnership with the U.S. Customs Service and U.S.P.I.S., NCMEC has received and processed more than 10,900 such leads. . . .

- In 1997 the Director of the FBI and I testified before the Senate Appropriations Subcommittee on Commerce, Justice, State and the Judiciary. The committee asked how serious was the problem of Internet-based child sexual exploitation. [Then FBI] Director [Louis] Freeh and I agreed that it was a serious and growing problem that we were just beginning to recognize and address, and that much more needed to be done at the federal, state and local levels. As a result of that hearing, Congress directed NCMEC to establish an Internet-based reporting mechanism for child pornography, online enticement of children, child molestation, child prostitution and child sex tourism. Congress also directed the Justice Department to establish multijurisdictional Internet Crimes Against Children Task Forces across the country.

- On March 9, 1998, NCMEC launched its new CyberTipline, www.cybertipline.com, the "911 for the Internet," to serve as the national online clearinghouse for investigative leads and tips regarding child sexual exploitation. NCMEC's CyberTipline is linked via server with the FBI, Customs Service and Postal Inspection Service. Leads are received and reviewed by NCMEC's analysts, who visit the reported sites, examine and evaluate the content, use search tools to try to identify perpetrators, and provide all lead information to the appropriate law enforcement agency and investigator. The FBI, Customs Service and Postal Inspection Service have "real time" access to the leads. Both the FBI and Customs Service have assigned agents who work directly out of NCMEC and review reports. The U.S. Secret Service has assigned three analysts who assist in the review and prioritization process. The results: to date, NCMEC has received and processed over 70,000 leads, 60,000 of which were reports of child pornography, resulting in hundreds of arrests and successful prosecutions.

- In December 1999, Congress passed the Protection of Children from Sexual Predators Act, mandating that Internet Service Providers [ISPs] and others report child pornography on their sites to law enforcement, with the ISPs subject to substantial fines for failure to report. Again, Congress asked NCMEC if it could handle the reports through its CyberTipline. NCMEC agreed. While the reporting mechanism is being formalized, NCMEC has entered into agreements with 85 major ISPs, including industry leaders America Online and the Microsoft Network, who are already reporting child pornography on their sites voluntarily.

Today, NCMEC is receiving hundreds of reports and tips regarding child pornography from across America and around the world each week, and it is pursuing those leads aggressively with the appropriate law enforcement agencies. Between March 1998 and April 2002, NCMEC received 93 child sex tourism leads, 789 child prostitution leads, and 2,358 non-family child sexual molestation leads.

We are proud of the progress. Following the Supreme Court's 1982 *Ferber v. New York* decision holding that child pornography was not protected speech, child pornography disappeared from the shelves of adult bookstores, the Customs Service launched an aggressive effort to intercept it as it entered the country, and the U.S. Postal Inspection Service cracked down on its distribution through the mails. However, child pornography did not disappear, it went underground. That lasted until the advent of the Internet, when those for whom child pornography was a way of life suddenly had a vehicle for networking, trading and communicating with like-minded individuals with virtual anonymity and little concern about apprehension. They could trade images with like-minded individuals, and in some cases even abuse children "live," while others watched via the Internet.

However, in recent years law enforcement began to catch up, and enforcement action came to the Internet. The FBI created its Innocent Images Task Force. The Customs Service expanded its activities through its CyberSmuggling Center. The Postal Inspection Service continued and enhanced its strong attack on child pornography. The Congress funded thirty Internet Crimes Against Children Task Forces at the state and local levels across the country. Child pornography prosecutions have increased an average of 10% per year in every year since 1995. We were making enormous progress.

The Dangers of Virtual Child Pornography

That is why we are so concerned about the impact of the Court's decision. We fear that this decision permits those who prey upon children to legally produce, possess and distribute sexually explicit images that are virtually indistinguishable from images of actual children. Increasingly, graphics software packages and computer animation are being used to manipulate or "morph" images and to create "virtual" images indistinguishable from photographic depictions of actual human beings. Not only will this enable continued victimization of actual children and fuel the growth of the child pornography market, but it severely impairs the ability of law enforcement and prosecutors to protect children by enforcing existing laws prohibiting such crimes.

NCMEC has been the national leader in the use of imaging technology for good. Our forensic artists are "aging" photos of long-term missing children, and performing facial re-constructions from morgue photos and skeletal remains of unidentified deceased children. These techniques keep long-term cases alive, generate new leads for police, and provide hope for searching parents. It is a powerful use of technology. However, the same technology can be used for evil as well.

Child pornography images are often used to exploit more children than just those seen in the image itself.

Examples of Virtual Child Pornography

It is already happening. [In April 2002], NCMEC received a child pornography report in which the image depicted a graphic sexual act between an adult male and what appeared to be an eight- or nine-year-old girl. One of NCMEC's Cyber-Tipline analysts recognized the child from a photo on a nudist site. The original photo of the child did not depict any sexual activity. In the new image, the pornographer had taken the child's image, cut it off at her waist, attached her body from the waist up to another photograph, and created a new image depicting the child being violated by an adult male.

That image still qualifies as child pornography under current law since the child is identifiable and will be harmed by the distribution of her image. Thus, the pornographer's next step is simply to make the child another child so that she is no longer identifiable. Alas, that now appears to be protected speech.

Recently, in California, an individual was arrested and convicted on molestation and child pornography charges. This individual took images of high-profile U.S. gymnasts (all under the age of 18) and, using computer technology, removed their leotards. He then added in genitalia and lewd poses. These images were then used to lower the inhibitions of a twelve-year-old girl whom he later molested. Technically, this is a "morphed" child pornography case. However, it does prove the point that the existence of child pornography images are often used to exploit more children than just those seen in the image itself.

One last example I'd like to offer is from a 1995 U.S. Postal Inspection Service investigation. The defendant in this case would first convince young girls to "model" for him by showing them pictures of young girls wearing only underwear. Then, progressively, he showed the children child pornography videotapes to lure them into a sexual relationship. The videotapes were produced in the 1980's and early 1990's (prior to the known morphing technology). The defendant was convicted and is now dead.

How can a police officer or prosecutor anywhere in America ascertain the true identity of the child? For the past two years, NCMEC has worked with state and local police to identify as many of these children as possible, and we continue to build that capacity. Since the child victims are local residents somewhere, and since these images are rapidly disseminated all over the world, working closely with local law enforcement is key to our ongoing process of identifying victims, enabling more prosecutions. However, it is very difficult, and [it is] clear that most children in child pornography are not identifiable. Based on the court's new standard, thousands of cases will not go forward.

Child Pornography Fuels Child Abuse

Child pornography is different, not like other kinds of speech. A decade ago, FBI Special Agent Ken Lanning, now retired, author of NCMEC's major publications in this field, outlined for Congress why pedophiles collect and distribute child pornography:

1. To justify their obsession for children

2. To stimulate their sexual drive

3. To lower a child's inhibitions

4. To preserve a child's youth

5. To blackmail

6. As a medium of exchange

7. For profit

As Agent Lanning noted, molesters use child pornography to stimulate their own desires and fuel their fantasies for children as sexual partners. Viewing these images whets the appetite of the molester and serves as a precursor to his own sexual acts with children. The more frequently a molester views child pornography, the more he, like his child victims, becomes desensitized to the abnormality of his conduct. He can convince himself that his behavior is normal, and eventually he will need more and increasingly explicit child pornography to satisfy his cravings. When mere visual stimulation no longer satisfies him, he will often progress to sexually molesting live children.

Child pornography is not just an aberrant form of free expression, it is a criminal tool, used to seduce and manipulate child victims, break down a child's inhibitions, and make sex between adults and children appear "normal." Just as we charge drug dealers with the possession of drug paraphernalia and would-be burglars with the possession of "burglary tools," so must we have the ability to limit the use of child pornography, a clear, unambiguous "molestation tool" for pedophiles and child molesters.

There is compelling evidence that visual depictions of sexually explicit conduct involving children cause real physical, emotional and psychological damage not only to depicted children but also to non-depicted children. It is just as insidious, whether it is a photographic record of a child's actual victimization, or a photographic depiction used as a tool or device to subsequently victimize other children. What will be the primary impacts of the Court's decision?

1. While the creation of purely "virtual" child pornography will increase dramatically, it now becomes more likely that predators will sexually victimize children and photograph the act. However, before distribution, they will use imaging techniques to morph and manipulate images to create a new identity for the child, thereby avoiding prosecution. We are already seeing perpetrators modify existing images to make them look more like "virtual" images.

2. Since determining the identity of children in child pornography is very difficult, oftentimes impossible, the requirement that a specific child be identified will result in thousands of prosecutions under child pornography law not happening.

3. Since advances in technology have made virtual child porn indistinguishable from actual child porn, in most cases it will be impossible for law enforcement and prosecutors to establish with certainty which is which.

4. Thousands of kids are going to be harmed as a result.

In conclusion, let me say that we do not believe that all is gloom and doom. We are encouraged and supportive about Attorney General [John] Ashcroft's commitment to use other statutes to aggressively prosecute these cases.

We are encouraged by the swift reaction from Congress. We believe that a new statute on this point is absolutely justified by the State's compelling interest in protecting children from the serious threat that child pornography, real or virtual, poses to their physical and mental health, safety and well-being.

The Government Should Help Parents Shield Children from Obscene and Violent Material

Kevin W. Saunders

Kevin W. Saunders is a professor at Michigan State University School of Law and the author of Saving Our Children from the First Amendment, *from which the following viewpoint is excerpted.*

> [A]t the confluence of two streams of concern which flow through our polity—our concern for the protection of our First Amendment freedoms and our concern for the protection of our children—we expect to hear a roar rather than a purr.

In 1949, [U.S. Supreme Court] Justice [Robert H.] Jackson wrote: "There is danger that, if the Court does not temper its doctrinaire logic with a little practical wisdom, it will convert the constitutional Bill of Rights into a suicide pact." Similarly, writing for the Court in 1963, Justice [Arthur] Goldberg stated: "[W]hile the Constitution protects against invasions of individual rights, it is not a suicide pact." The position that the Constitution is not a suicide pact finds support in other opinions of the Supreme Court and lower courts.

Yet, how better for a society to commit suicide than to fail in its duty to raise its youth in a safe and psychologically healthy manner? We are so failing. While rates fluctuate, violent crime by youths is unacceptably high. Homicide is the second leading cause of death for fifteen to twenty-four-year-olds and the leading cause among African American males of that age. Teenage pregnancy rates are also too high. Although down 11 percent from its 1994 high, the birthrate for unwed fifteen- to nineteen-year-olds was 41.5 births per thousand in 1998. Children also use tobacco and alcohol at unacceptable rates. The Campaign for Tobacco-Free Kids cites government reports showing that more than 5 million children are current smokers, and 43.8 percent of high school boys used tobacco in the month preceding a 2001 survey. The Campaign for Alcohol Free Kids reports that 10 million American teenagers drink monthly; 8 million drink weekly, with half a million of those binge drinking; that alcohol consumption is not uncommon at ages eleven and twelve; and that a majority of grade five through twelve students say that advertising encourages them to drink. We are failing in our duty to society and its coming generations, and the First Amendment's limitations on our ability to restrict the influences children face are among the roots of that failure.

The First Amendment does contain the most important of our political freedoms. Stating those freedoms very succinctly, the amendment says: "Congress shall make no law respecting an establishment of religion, or prohibiting the free exercise thereof; or abridging the freedom of speech, or of the press; or the right of the people peaceably to assemble, and to petition the Government for a redress of grievances." The importance of the amendment to adults is obvious, but its importance to children is less clear. Even if children should enjoy some First Amendment rights, the benefits these rights provide may well be limited by a child's developmental stage. Rather than concluding that the rights of children and adults should be equal, we should consider the possibility of limiting children's rights to correspond to children's capacities.

Shielding Children from Harmful Speech

Free expression also has its costs. While there are limitations on adult expression, those limitations are narrow. Only when a clear and present danger attends the speech or when the speech falls within certain categories—obscenity, fighting words or libel—may adult speech be limited. When the recipient of the speech is a child still developing psychologically, the costs of unrestrained speech may be too high. Shielding children from harms that adults may have to tolerate protects children in their development. This same shielding also serves to protect the rest of society. Any negative effects that free expression has on children affect not only children but society as a whole.

Society should be allowed to limit the access of children to materials not suitable to their age.

The thesis of this work is that the First Amendment should function differently for children and for adults. For communication among adults the amendment should be fully robust, perhaps even more so than under current law. Where children are concerned, however, the amendment should be significantly weaker. Society should be allowed to limit the access of children to materials not suitable to their age. Legal prohibitions on distributing sexual materials to children are now constitutional, and this treatment should extend to violent materials, vulgar or profane materials, and the hate-filled music used to recruit the next generation to supremacist organizations. No good reason requires that we recognize a right on the part of children to such access. Nor should the free-expression rights of adults be seen as including a right to express themselves to the children of others. The full development and autonomy of adults may require the right to express themselves on a wide variety of topics, but that right should not include access to children who are not their own. Perhaps no one should tell authors, producers or computer programmers what they can create. But that is not the same as saying that they have a right to a juvenile audience for their books, films or video games.

The Specter of Censorship

The immediate response to this thesis is certain to be, "Isn't that censorship?" Yes, it is. But, is censorship always an evil? Even with adults, there are arguments that censorship is sometimes positive. Some feminists argue that the harm pornography does to women outweighs the free-expression rights of the producers and even adult consumers of pornography. Advertising tobacco and alcohol causes harm, even if the ads could be restricted to adults, and advertising prescription drugs to the end consumer increases the cost of health care and may cause needless danger to those consumers. Hate speech, even when directed toward adults, may have strongly negative effects on those adults, even having medical consequences.

These are real costs to free expression. For adults, however, the costs are worth bearing. The lines between hate speech and the advocacy of a political position may be too difficult to draw to allow a prohibition on such speech. Commercial speech also has value. Consumers need to know the differences among products or the varying prices of the goods they purchase. Not only men, but women and couples may use pornography, and the right to obtain such material and for the producers to express themselves may be worth retaining. Generally, the dangers of government censorship provide reason to treat with skepticism any efforts to censor communication among adults. Even if some censorship might have overall positive value, the great dangers of censorship to political freedom, the attainment of truth and autonomy rights justify a strong freedom of expression that includes a strong presumption against censorship.

Children, however, are different. The values behind the First Amendment that make the costs worth bearing are not as strong when children are involved. The costs are also greater. Children are in the process of development. Influences that might be minor for adults can have a seriously negative impact on children. The lessened benefits of free expression for or toward children and the greater costs attendant to such expression reduce the strength of the presumption against all censorship and should leave open the possibility of providing more protection for children. . . .

While society benefits . . . from the strong free-expression rights it recognizes for adults, the benefits are simply not as strong in allowing equivalent free expression for children.

The Marketplace of Ideas

Justice [Oliver Wendell] Holmes explained his view of the theory behind the First Amendment's speech and press clause in *Abrams v. United States*. Holmes recognized the desire to suppress the expression of opinion regarded as incorrect, but he questioned the reasonableness of the surety with which the determination of truth or falsity can be made.

> [W]hen men have realized that time has upset many fighting faiths, they may come to believe even more than they believe the very foundations of their own conduct that the ultimate good desired is better reached by free trade in ideas—that the best test of truth is the power of thought to get itself accepted in the competition of the market, and that truth is the only ground upon which their wishes safely can be carried out. That at any rate is the theory of our Constitution.

Holmes's "marketplace of ideas" justification for the freedoms of speech and of the press reflects that offered by [British philosopher] John Stuart Mill in his 1859 work *On Liberty*. While other theories also explain or justify the protection given expression . . . this "marketplace of ideas" has a firm historical basis.

This theory's central import to the political process is reason enough to maintain a strong freedom of expression, but it is most clearly of importance for those who are actual participants in the political system. If children are not allowed to vote, this rationale at least partially evaporates. Adults who wish to influence political or social change should direct their efforts to other adults, those who can vote for that change. Children should be influenced by their parents and by society, with the role of other adults limited to trying to affect the political community in its decisions on the influences to which children will be exposed. Expression by children, as it relates to social and political change, may have value, but again its value must be less than that of adults, or there would be no justification for denying children the vote....

None of [the rationales for free expression] speak particularly strongly to children. While society benefits, despite occasional costs, from the strong free-expression rights it recognizes for adults, the benefits are simply not as strong in allowing equivalent free expression for children, either in their own communication or in the information they receive from adults other than their own parents or guardians.

Costs of Free Expression

The desire to censor is, of course, based on the perceived costs of expression. But, even where the freedoms of speech and press have their costs, the benefits may clearly outweigh those costs. For example, excesses by the press may be criticized. Sensational headlines may sell papers but may also inaccurately attribute behavior to an individual damaging the person's reputation. At least for public officials, the cost is worth bearing, and plaintiffs must show not only falsity but that the media organ knew of that falsity or recklessly disregarded a known risk that the report was false. A public official may then have to tolerate false reports that injure his or her reputation, but the failure to protect the press would have significant negative effects. The press, faced with potential liability, would not report on public officials unless they were very sure of their news gathering. The public would be deprived of reports that might be both true and very relevant to voting decisions and public accountability. Where a public official is involved, the balance runs in favor of protecting the public's need to know, even in the face of some possible cost to that official.

In other situations, the benefits may not as clearly outweigh the costs. It has been argued that pornography exposes women to unequal treatment. Hate speech, either on the basis of race or gender, has been said to have similar effects. Violence in media depictions may be argued to lead to violence in the real world. Campaign contributions, seen as a protected expression of opinion, may have a corrupting effect on the political process. The Internet, in opening channels of communications among adults, may expose children to material that is certainly inappropriate and may be damaging. Advertising may mislead consumers. Protection of profane speech and shock media may have a coarsening effect on society. . . .

Generally the balance has been properly struck in favor of providing First-Amendment protection. In some cases the benefits outweigh recognized costs. In other cases, fear that difficulties in drawing lines aimed at eliminating speech with little or no value would lead to the suppression of speech that has value and ought to be protected for its own sake limits the inclination to regulate. This, for example, is sometimes offered as a rationale for the protection of shock media. While there may be little value other than that some find such programming entertaining, once limits are imposed on shock media, where is the line to be drawn? Where is the cut to be made along the continuum ranging from programs that present shocking material for purely entertainment purposes, at one end, through confrontational reporting and on to the evening news, at the other?

Concern over drawing lines is less compelling where children are involved. This is particularly so if parents retain the right to second-guess society and make available to their children materials that others may not provide them directly. Furthermore, the costs of free expression are experienced more through their effects on children than on adults. Reducing those costs by imposing limitations only in this area of primary negative effect can benefit society while leaving the greatest benefits, adult-to-adult communication, free.

Children may be more affected by material such as pornography or depictions of violence.

Harms to Children

Children are different. Their abilities to analyze conflicting visions of society are not fully developed. While we may believe that through free and open exchange adults will eventually arrive at the truth, the argument is not as convincing for children. Without the experiential basis of adults, children are more likely to be led astray. And, we may be more confident in the fact that the direction is, in fact, wrong. While it may be unreasonable to claim general infallibility, it is more reasonable to claim a better grasp of the situation than that enjoyed by children.

The harms done by speech or press protected by the First Amendment may also be more severe when children are exposed to objectionable expression. Children may be more affected by material such as pornography or depictions of violence. Those in the process of developing psychologically may have that development harmed by depictions that would not negatively affect adults. Certainly, the child's beliefs as to the violence present in the world or of the variety of sexual activity practiced by the average adult may, in the absence of real life experience, be affected by a view of the world formed primarily through television and the movies.

John Stuart Mill himself, the champion of freedom of expression and strong proponent of libertarianism, recognized that children may be treated differently. Mill was willing to allow society to shape the thinking of children in a way that would be unacceptable for adults. In considering possible rationales for society acting paternalistically toward adults, Mill agreed that punishment for the sake of the actor is preferable to punishment for failure to provide benefits to society. But, he said that society has other ways of bringing its "weaker members" up to the expected standards of conduct. Mill noted that society has power over these "weaker members" during their youth and may attempt, in that period, to teach them rational conduct. Mill recognized the primary role of parents in raising their children but concluded that, when parents fail to provide training, the state has a role to play.

Society has the right and duty to limit the access of adults to other people's children.

The period of childhood is that in which, even for Mill, society has the opportunity to teach the values it hopes children will accept as they become adults. Teaching opposing values to children would defeat society's right to educate. Children simply do not have the competency to determine which of the competing theories of values is preferable. That is not to say that there cannot be debate over values, but it is one that must occur on an adult level. Adult expression of opinion over the values to teach children should be robust and open, but not all the proponents of competing positions should have access to society's children. Parents, of course, play a primary role in teaching values, and society should not punish parents for teaching values that disagree with those of the majority. But that does not mean that society must leave children at the mercy of all others who wish to teach children values that differ from those of the majority and of their parents. Society has the right and duty to limit the access of adults to other people's children.

The Role of Parents

The second response to the thesis that society has a role in the protection of children from expression that may be harmful to them is likely to be, "Shouldn't that be the job of parents?" Again, yes it should. Not only should parents have the right to control the influences to which their children are exposed, it is a part of the job of parenting. But parents need help in discharging that responsibility. It may have been easy to make sure that children were exposed to the right influences in an earlier era. Children are now subjected to far more influences, from videos to cable television to video games to the Internet, than when the issues were simply what books to read or which of the television network broadcasts to watch. The greater explicitness of both sex and violence in the current media also make the concern over inappropriate exposure far more pressing.

That this is the parents' job does not mean that the state has no role. It only means that the governmental role should be a supportive role rather than one that supplants the parents as the determiner of the values to which children are exposed. The decisions the government makes will have an effect on the child's ability to obtain exposure to various forms of media, but it should only be an effect on third parties' direct provision of these products to the child. Parents must still be allowed to disagree with the state, purchase the material and provide it to their children themselves.

Harmful Speech Is Like Cigarettes

To conclude that, because controlling the influences on children is the parents' job, the state should have no such role is unreasonable. Consider a similar argument for cigarettes. It should also be the parents' job to teach their children not to smoke. But from that premise, no one would argue that the state should not be allowed to prohibit sales of tobacco to minors. Parents need the support of the state in their efforts. While tobacco laws may not assure that children will not smoke, making it more difficult to purchase cigarettes provides at least some help to parents.

The response to that is likely to be that expression is different. While the Constitution does not protect cigarette smoking, the First Amendment does protect the freedom of expression. Expression is, admittedly, different. Values behind free expression are not just different but more important than any values behind letting people make their own choices regarding the consumption of tobacco. Nonetheless, as just discussed, the values of free expression are less when children are concerned. This is most clear for the autonomy interests represented by the guarantees of free expression. Even if one accepts that one value behind the First Amendment is allowing the individual to be the person he or she wants to be, that does not mean that such a laissez-faire attitude toward children is appropriate. If children were to be allowed the same autonomy rights as adults, that would seem to extend to tobacco use. There are differences in the sort of harm caused, but cigarettes and violent media both cause harm: the health associations, such as the American Medical Association, and the surgeon general have found this to be true, and the disagreement over that point in both cases comes primarily from the industries themselves.

Children's Political Education

The major difference between the tobacco and free expression issues, with regard to the rights of children or of nonparental adults with regard to children, is in what occurs when the child reaches the age of majority. When the child turns eighteen, there is no sudden need for the new adult to be a competent smoker. Thus, the child need not be a smoker in training. On turning eighteen, however, the child is suddenly a member of the voting part of the political community, and it is necessary that the new adult be a competent voter. Exposure to political debate and the issues that face the community are then needed, at least during the latter part of the individual's minority.

The need for children to learn about politics does not mean that society must throw up its hands and allow children to experience all possible forms of expression. It is a part of our tradition that parents are primarily responsible for instilling values in their children, and we must recognize that such influence is likely to carry over to the choices of young voters. It should only be the influences of government, as they affect the future voting choices of children, that should raise concern. That influence is likely to come through the schools, and it is there that caution should be exercised. Limitations on video tapes and games or the music children can purchase directly are of less concern, since parents can obtain any material they believe appropriate. Schools, however, could be used to inculcate values that the parent finds objectionable. They could be used to skew the political process. If the schools take one side on a political issue, children whose parents are on that side will have their values reinforced. Children whose parents are on the opposite side will have the values their parents are trying to inculcate called into question. One side may then be able to use the schools to help implant its political position in the upcoming generation of voters.

This concern over the political savvy of the next generation does not mean that there can be no limitations on speech to children. Limitations that do not absolutely prohibit all exposure of children to legal, such as nonobscene, expression should be acceptable. If the only limits are on direct sales, parents can still obtain materials they think suitable for their children, even if society disagrees. The only change such a regulation mandates is a sort of change in presumption. Without such limits, the presumption seems to be that it is acceptable for children to have access to the material, but this presumption is at least theoretically rebuttable by the parent who tells a child not to purchase a particular CD or see a particular film. With limitations, the presumption is that children should not watch, read, listen to or play particular material, but again the presumption is rebuttable by the parent who provides the material for his or her child.

Again, the issue of speech limitations in school is more serious. Care must be taken that the societal political debate is not skewed. But even here, it does not mean that all regulation is foreclosed. Limits on sexual indecency certainly are allowed, but the schools should not shut off one of the two positions on the political debate over whether obscene material should be proscribed. Limits on speech that degrades another person on the basis of race, color or gender should be allowed, but the debate on affirmative action should not be skewed. Discussion of war, crime or the First Amendment should be vital, but that does not mean that violent video games must be allowed in the cafeteria, even if the school allows nonviolent games.

There are serious concerns over negative media effects on children.

A Matter of Common Sense?

The suggested likely first responses already discussed would have come from those who disagree with the proposed thesis, but there is also a dismissive response that could come from a supporter. That response would be: "They're only children. Of course their First Amendment rights are different from those of adults. Isn't that just common sense?" The answer, as with the answers to the "Isn't that censorship?" and "Isn't that the parents' job?" is again "Yes." But, common sense and the dictates of the law, including the Constitution, are not always the same thing, and there are certainly interpretations of the First Amendment that are contrary to the position taken here.

The American Civil Liberties Union [ACLU] has consistently taken a contrary position. Sometimes, as in the case of the Communications Decency Act's attempt to prevent minors from accessing indecent material on the Internet, the legal claims of those who, along with the ACLU, successfully sought to enjoin the act, were based at least in part on the effect the attempt to shield minors would have on the access rights of adults. But, even when adult access has not been threatened, the ACLU has taken positions against measures intended to protect minors. The v-chip was criticized as a variety of censorship that violates the First Amendment. The ACLU argued that the v-chip legislation was a "governmental usurpation of parental control" over what their children see on television, despite the fact that parents were not required to activate the filter. If they wanted help in limiting their children's viewing, the scheme provided that opportunity, while parents who were less concerned with media violence could simply choose not to avail themselves of the aid the v-chip would provide.

The ACLU was similarly unimpressed by efforts to label musical recordings to warn parents of objectionable content. Once again, some of the concern regarded the likelihood that retail chains would opt not to carry recordings labeled as unsuitable for minors and the negative effect this would have on adult access. But the organization also generally questioned the wisdom of shielding children, saying "scapegoating artistic expression as a cause of social ills is simplistic. How can serious social problems like violent crime, racism or suicide be solved by covering children's ears?" Despite this skepticism, there are serious concerns over negative media effects on children, and once again, the labeling would not prohibit parents who do not share that concern from providing labeled recordings to their children. Parents would simply be provided the information necessary to make an informed decision.

Children's Intellectual Freedom

The American Library Association has taken a similar position regarding attempts to require filtering on computers in schools and libraries that received federal funding to provide Internet access. Again, the concern was not solely that adults might lose access to valuable material on the Internet. In an explanation of their concerns, the association said: "People of all ages and backgrounds come to libraries seeking connection to a world of ideas via books, magazines and the Internet. Providing access to the broadest spectrum of information possible is the heart of America's public libraries."

Probably the strongest assertion of the expression rights of minors may be found in Marjorie Heins's . . . book, *Not in Front of the Children*. Heins is a free-expression activist, former ACLU litigator and current director of the Free Expression Policy Project of the National Coalition Against Censorship. She describes, as a major theme of her book, "the intellectual freedom interests of young people . . . a concept too often impatiently dismissed by child protectionists[, who think m]inors insufficiently mature or socialized to understand and resist the ideas that a majority of adults think are not good for them." She goes on to question the wisdom of this protectionist approach:

> But is this really the best way to prepare youngsters for adult life in a democratic society? The simultaneous titillation, anxiety, and confusion spawned by forbidden speech zones may do more harm than good. Certainly healthy upbringing, education and community values are likelier than taboos to immunize them against violent, degrading, or simpleminded ideas. Censorship may also frustrate young people's developing sense of autonomy and self-respect, and increase their feelings of alienation. Some older children and

adolescents are able to process information and make coherent decisions at the same level as many adults. They *need* access to information and ideas precisely because they are in the process [of] becoming functioning members of society and cannot do so if they are kept in ideological blinders until they are 18.

But younger children clearly are insufficiently mature to understand what is good for them. A very young child is unlikely to understand sound nutrition and may need to be told that a diet consisting entirely of fast food is unacceptable and to eat his or her vegetables, whatever this may do to a "developing sense of autonomy." While the negative effects of certain expressive influences may be less clear, they do exist and children should be shielded. Parents are in the best position to recognize the developing good sense of their children, and their judgment should be backed up by the sort of restrictions advocated here, which leave those parents free to provide materials that may not be directly available to children. If it is accepted that younger children should be protected, the issue is simply one of where to draw the line. If Heins's argument is only that children should not be shielded right up until their eighteenth birthdays, there is some strength to the position. . . .

Legal Precedents

Turning to the legal precedents, support in opposition to the thesis of this work is also available, although . . . those precedents, at least at the highest level, are not dispositive. The first important case in this line is *Tinker v. Des Moines School Dist.* . . . *Tinker*, in recognizing First Amendment protection for student arm bands worn in school in protest of United States actions in Southeast Asia, said, "First Amendment rights, applied in light of the special characteristics of the school environment, are available to teachers and students. It can hardly be argued that either students or teachers shed their constitutional rights to freedom of speech or expression at the schoolhouse gate." In a later case, *Erznoznik v. Jacksonville*, striking down a ban on nudity in films visible from the street, as at a drive-in movie, the Court again recognized First Amendment rights of minors but also recognized that those rights are weaker than those of adults. The Court said: "It is well settled that a State or municipality can adopt more stringent controls on communicative materials available to youths than on those available to adults. Nevertheless, minors are entitled to a significant measure of First Amendment protections, and only in relatively narrow and well-defined circumstances may government bar public dissemination of protected material to them."

The *Tinker* case is an important recognition of expression rights involving children, but it must be recognized that the issue there was political speech that should enjoy the strongest protection. The promised later treatment of the case must be sensitive to that variety of speech even though arguing for, as recognized by later cases on schools and expression, lesser expression rights where children are concerned. *Erznoznik* is also of limited application. The Court had already recognized, in *Ginsberg v. New York*, that a lesser level of sexuality will justify bans on dissemination to children, as obscene for that audience, of materials that would not be obscene when distributed to adults. *Erznoznik* concluded that not all nudity, potentially reaching "a picture of a baby's buttocks, the nude body of a war victim, or scenes from a culture in which nudity is indigenous," rather than solely sexually explicit nudity, is swept within the state interest recognized in *Ginsberg*. Nor could the Court find any other governmental interest that would justify the ban. There is, however, additional language that is contrary to the position taken here. The Court said that speech "cannot be suppressed solely to protect the young from ideas or images that a legislative body thinks unsuitable for them. In most circumstances, the values protected by the First Amendment are no less applicable when government seeks to control the flow of information to minors."

Preparing Children to Be Voters

A more recent lower court decision recognized free expression rights of children with a vengeance, or at least with a strong use of rhetorical hyperbole. *American Amusement Machines Ass'n v. Kendrick* enjoined the enforcement of an Indianapolis ordinance limiting the ability of minors to play violent games in video arcades without a parent or guardian present. Judge [Richard] Posner, writing for the three-judge panel, said:

> Children have First Amendment rights. . . . This is not merely a matter of pressing the First Amendment to a dryly logical extreme. The murderous fanaticism displayed by young German soldiers in World War II, alumni of the Hitler Jugend, illustrates the danger of allowing government to control the access of children to information and opinion. Now that eighteen-year-olds have the right to vote, it is obvious that they must be allowed the freedom to form their political views on the basis of uncensored speech *before* they turn eighteen, so that their minds are not a blank when they first exercise the franchise. And since an eighteen-year-old's right to vote is a right personal to him rather than a right to be exercised on his behalf by his parents, the right of parents to enlist the aid of the state to shield their children from ideas of which the parents disapprove cannot be plenary either. People are unlikely to become well-functioning independent-minded adults and responsible citizens if they are raised in an intellectual bubble.

This view seems in conflict with that of the Supreme Court. In *Ginsberg* the Court found two state interests that justified the limitations on selling indecent material to minors. The second of the two was the state's interest in the well-being of its youth. The first was the interest of parents. The Court said "constitutional interpretation has consistently recognized that the parents' claim to authority in their own household to direct the rearing of their children is basic in the structure of our society" and that parents are entitled to the support of the laws in discharging their responsibility. It is true that *Ginsberg* addressed sexual material, but the interest cited was not limited to sex. If children have independent First Amendment rights, the *Ginsberg* result might still be reached by concluding that the material was obscene when viewed by children, a conclusion the Court did reach, but the interests of the parents would not have been relevant to that conclusion. The Court clearly recognized the rights of parents to determine that material is inappropriate for their children, and that is a far cry from children having fully independent rights under the First Amendment.

On the other hand, Judge Posner does point to a real issue regarding older minors, and if his analysis were limited to that concern, his view may not as directly conflict with *Ginsberg*. While *Ginsberg* recognized parental rights to control the influences their children confront, the statute at issue there addressed distribution to children under seventeen. The statute in *Ginsberg* had also been enacted in an era in which eighteen-year-olds did not have the right to vote. With the eighteen-year-old vote and the Indianapolis statute's extension to all those under eighteen, Posner's concern carries more weight. While it may be difficult to argue with a straight face that playing violent video games is necessary to casting an intelligent vote, the line between political speech and entertainment has been recognized as difficult to draw. Despite the rhetoric and the specter of Nazis emerging due to efforts to limit the exposure of children to objectionable media influences, Judge Posner's concern does point to the possibility that an age below full adulthood should be taken as the point at which expanded, or perhaps full, First Amendment rights are enjoyed.

Indecent Broadcasts Should Not Be Censored

Marjorie Heins

Marjorie Heins is the coordinator of the Free Expression Policy Project of the Brennan Center for Justice at the New York University School of Law.

The Federal Communications Commission [FCC] laid down the gauntlet [in March 2006] with a blistering volume of new decisions that condemn a dozen TV shows for "indecency," profanity, or both. The question now is whether anyone will take up the challenge and ask a court of law to rule on the constitutionality of the agency's sweeping assertion of power to censor broadcasting.

The new indecency fines total more than $4 million, which is more, according to *Broadcasting & Cable* magazine, than all the TV shows that have previously been fined for indecency put together. (Most previous fines were against radio, not television.) The targets ranged from the famous Super Bowl "wardrobe malfunction" of 2004 to the punishment of a California educational TV station for broadcasting the PBS documentary *The Blues*, directed by Martin Scorsese.

Among the more striking rulings were:

- Scorsese's documentary, which includes interviews of blues musicians, is indecent and profane because the musicians use variations on what the Commission delicately describes as the "F-word" and the "S-word." *The Blues*, according to our federal culture czars, does not fit within the *Saving Private Ryan* exception that they have developed for situations where deleting swear words "would have altered the nature of the artistic

Marjorie Heins, "America's Culture Czars," *The Free Expression Policy Project*, March 21, 2006. Reproduced by permission.

work and diminished the power, realism, and immediacy of the film experience." Scorsese's artistic purpose, say the FCC commissioners, could have been fulfilled "without the repeated broadcast of expletives."

• The term "bullshit" is profane and indecent, but "dickhead" is not (both were heard on an episode of *NYPD Blue*). The hairsplitting here makes for humorous reading, until one realizes that this is our government suppressing words and ideas that are protected by the First Amendment.

History of the Broadcast Indecency Standard

The FCC's power to suppress whatever it considers indecent in broadcast television and radio—but not in cable, satellite, print, or cyberspace—derives from a combination of political and historical circumstances. Because the airwaves are a public resource, and broadcast licenses are thought to be a public trust, courts and Congress have long assumed that broadcasting gets less First Amendment protection than other media. In the 1970s, when the Supreme Court upheld the FCC's power to censor "indecency" in the famous "seven dirty words" case (*FCC v. Pacifica*), perhaps it seemed natural that there should be some extra restraints—beyond the obscenity law that applies to everyone—on the immensely popular, pervasive, and powerful mass medium known as broadcasting.

The Supreme Court in the *Pacifica* case seized on the "invasiveness" of the medium, and its ready accessibility to children, as extra reasons to allow government censorship of what was clearly First Amendment–protected expression. But of course, many media are "invasive" and accessible to children, and in the near-30 years since *Pacifica*, the arrival of cable, satellite, and the Internet have made the FCC's censorship of the airwaves even more anomalous and constitutionally suspect than before. Some argue that this means the FCC's broad and vague "indecency" standard (which has now been supplemented by separate rulings on "profanity") should extend to cable and satellite as well. But Congress and the FCC know this would be unconstitutional, and for good reason: the specter of such a far-reaching government censorship scheme would turn the First Amendment upside-down.

Meanwhile, the FCC continues to levy fines and lay down cultural judgments about traditional broadcast programming, without its censorship decisions being tested in court. How do they manage this feat? How do they get away with telling Martin Scorsese or the directors of *NYPD Blue* that their artistic choices are wrong?

The agency's power over license renewals and transfers means that broadcasters rarely want to challenge indecency rulings in court. Media companies may rattle their sabers, but at the end of the day, they usually settle with the Commission. In one instance back in the 1990s when a radio company (Evergreen Media) did go to court, it ended up settling in exchange for what turned out to be an empty promise by the Commission to put greater specificity into its indecency definition.

The problem, of course, is that the definition turns on what is "patently offensive" according to "contemporary community standards for the broadcast medium." It's hard to get much less specific than that.

[The government] should not have ... any role at all in suppressing constitutionally protected words, ideas, or images that five politically appointed commissioners decide are offensive.

FCC Procedures for Fining Broadcasters

In addition, the Commission levies its fines by way of a procedure called a Notice of Apparent Liability, or "NAL." Broadcasters faced with an NAL must challenge it through the agency's appeals process before going to court. And this appeals process can take years. Even after the appeal is decided, the broadcaster is supposed to wait for the Department of Justice to bring an action to collect the fine rather than seeking judicial review directly.

One artist whose work was deemed indecent by our cultural commissars a few years ago did take the FCC to court, but her case was dismissed on the ground that an appeal of the indecency ruling was still pending at the agency. Rap and performance artist Sarah Jones wasn't even a party to the FCC proceeding, but her song "Your Revolution"—an earthy critique of misogynist male rappers—had been deemed indecent by the tone-deaf FCC in 2001. Jones appealed the dismissal of her federal court case, but, just coincidentally, the agency rendered its own decision on appeal right before the government was due to file its brief in the federal appellate court. Now, the FCC said, "Your Revolution" isn't indecent after all. This fortuitously-timed ruling was clearly designed to "moot" the federal court case, and leave the FCC free once more to police the airwaves for subversive words and naughty thoughts.

This is not to say that our government should have no role in regulating broadcasting—or other elements of the mass media, for that matter. Just as the consolidation of media ownership inevitably limits the range of available reporting, analysis, and entertainment, so decisions on how broadcast frequencies are used profoundly affect Americans' ability to exchange ideas and get the information they need to function as citizens of a democracy. The government therefore has an important structural role in assuring that diverse voices—not all of them large and for-profit—get to communicate over the air. What it should not have is any role at all in suppressing constitutionally protected words, ideas, or images that five politically appointed commissioners decide are offensive.

Both CBS and NBC have vowed to challenge these new rulings in court, but it remains to be seen whether their current intent will survive administrative agency attrition, politics, and the need to stay in the FCC's good graces.

FCC commissioners frequently write separate statements when releasing high-profile rulings. Commissioner Jonathan Adelstein took the opportunity to warn of the constitutional dangers lurking in the agency's most recent decisions. By abandoning a more "restrained enforcement policy," he said, the Commission "endangers the very authority we so delicately retain to enforce broadcast indecency rules." Translation: some of these latest rulings are so radical that they beg for not only a judicial reversal, but a judicial re-thinking of the entire FCC censorship regime.

Let us hope that if not CBS and NBC, then Martin Scorsese will have the wherewithal to go to court and rein in this renegade bureaucracy.

Libraries Should Not Use Internet Filters to Block Pornography

Daniel H. Bromberg

Daniel H. Bromberg is a lawyer for the Online Policy Group, a not-for-profit organization that works to ensure the privacy and civil rights of Internet users.

The Children's Internet Protection Act ("CIPA") requires libraries participating in certain federal funding programs to block Internet access to visual depictions that are obscene, child pornography, or (in some circumstances) harmful to minors through a particular method: the use of a "technology protection measure." Although the Act defines the term "technology protection measure," it offers no guidance on how such measures should distinguish between the low-value speech banned by CIPA and other speech on the Internet that is entitled to full First Amendment protection. Instead, CIPA simply defines a "technology protection measure" as a "specific technology that blocks or filters Internet access." This blind faith in technology is badly—and dangerously—misplaced. . . .

CIPA Forces Libraries to Use Blocking Software

To comply with CIPA, libraries that wish to provide their patrons with broad access to the Internet are forced, as a practical matter, to rely upon commercial blocking software. The Internet is massive. In 1997, it consisted of approximately 9.4 million host computers used by over 40 million people. As of September 2001, the number of people using the Internet had

Daniel H. Bromberg, *Brief of Amici Curia Online Policy Group, Inc., and Seth Finkelstein in Support of the Appellees, United States v. American Library Association*, Online Policy Group, 2003. Reproduced by permission.

expanded tenfold to at least 400 million, including approximately 143 million in the United States alone. Moreover, by that time, the rapidly expanding Internet had over 11 million unique "web" sites with more than two billion web pages reachable through ordinary search engines. Libraries do not have the technological capacity or expertise to write software that can filter through such a vast store of information and determine which sites contain visual depictions that are obscene, child pornography, or harmful to minors. As a consequence, libraries that are not content to provide their patrons with access to only a small number of pre-screened sites are generally forced to rely upon commercially developed blocking software, also sometimes known as "censorware," to comply with CIPA's "technology protection measure" requirement.

Commercial blocking software is not designed to comply with governmental obligations under the First Amendment.

Although the Government correctly points out that commercial blocking software permits users to "unblock" specific sites, libraries in fact have little ability to customize blocking software. Blocking software typically prohibits Internet users from accessing any domain name or Internet Protocol address that is contained on "control lists" compiled by the software's vendor. Software companies do not, however, reveal how these control lists are compiled. To the contrary, the companies treat the heuristics and other methods they use as well as the lists of sites that those methods generate as proprietary information, which they do not reveal to libraries and other consumers. Moreover, while users can unblock particular sites, it is impossible for a user to personalize blocking software in any significant manner because the control lists compiled by blocking companies typically contain hundreds of thousands of sites, and the Internet is ever-expanding. Thus, libraries that purchase blocking software effectively cede to their software vendors the decision about which sites to block.

Commercial Blocking Software Overregulates Speech

The abdication of decision-making responsibility to the creators of commercial blocking software required by CIPA poses great danger of unnecessary suppression of speech and viewpoint discrimination.

Commercial Blocking Software Purposefully Blocks Protected Speech Commercial blocking software typically permits consumers to block several dozen categories of Internet content. There is, however, "no category definition used by filtering software companies [that] is identical to CIPA's definitions of visual depictions that are obscene, child pornography, or harmful to minors." Indeed, commercial blocking software does not even offer categories limited to obscenity, child pornography, or visual depictions that are harmful to minors. The closest approximations are categories such as "Adult Material," "Adults Only," "Adult/Sexually Explicit," "Extreme/Obscene/Violence," "Pornography," "Sex," "Kids' Sites," "For Kids," "Illegal/Questionable," "Tasteless," and "Tasteless/Gross."

This omission is not surprising. Commercial blocking software is not designed to comply with governmental obligations under the First Amendment. Like any commercial product, blocking software is designed to satisfy the market's primary customers, which in the case of blocking software are parents who want to protect their children from all sexually explicit material, businesses that want to keep their employees focused on work and maintain a hospitable atmosphere in the office, and religious groups that want to spare their members exposure to material that offends their values. For example, one blocking-software company provides services to several religious Internet service providers and web sites, such as Christianity.com, Christian.net, and Crosswalk.com. Another company provides blocking services to 711.net/Global Internet Ministries, Christian Purity, and What Would Jesus View. And a third company offers a product that the American Family Association has repackaged as the "American Family Filter" and described as "built on the Christian princip[le] of holiness."

Commercial Blocking Software Is Inherently Overbroad Blocking-software vendors have an economic incentive to err on the side of overblocking. When a consumer is improperly denied access to a Web site by blocking software, he is unlikely to know that he has been denied access to anything of value and therefore is unlikely to become upset. By contrast, when a sexually graphic image appears on the screen of a consumer who has attempted to block such material, there is a good chance that the consumer will become incensed and complain to his blocking-software vendor. . . . (Libraries "tend to receive many more complaints from parents and the community about sites that are not filtered (i.e., complaints about underblocking) than about sites that are filtered improperly (i.e., complaints about overblocking)"). As a consequence, companies offering blocking software have a natural "desire to 'err on the side of caution' by screening out material that might be offensive to some customers." . . .

There is evidence that . . . blocking software routinely denies access to gay and lesbian sites that contain core political speech.

In addition, . . . institutions regularly engaged in suppressing speech tend to develop a bias in favor of suppression. When a "framework creates an agency or establishes an official charged particularly with reviewing speech," it "breed[s] an 'expertise' tending to favor censorship over speech." ("Because the censor's business is to censor, there inheres the danger that he may well be less responsive than a court—part of an independent branch of government—to the constitutionally protected interests in free expression.") For this reason as well, commercially developed blocking software has an inherent tendency to block more speech than necessary.

Commercial Blocking Software May Facilitate Viewpoint Discrimination There is also reason to fear that commercially developed blocking software will systematically discriminate against certain viewpoints. Although the heuristics employed by blocking software are generally unknown, *amici* [advisors to the court who are not parties to the litigation; referring here to the authors] are aware of one product that used the presence of words such as "lesbian," "gay," and "homosexual" in identifying sites dealing with sexuality. That product assigned points to particular words or phrases based on the inherent offensiveness of the word and its context. It treated the words "lesbian" and "homosexual" as inherently offensive, and for each appearance of those words a Web page received five points; sites accumulating 50 points were normally blocked. Words like "lesbian" and "homosexual," however, are likely to appear dozens of times in sites that discuss social and political issues of concern to the lesbian and gay communities, but have little to do with sexuality, much less obscenity and pornography. Thus, under the heuristics employed by this company, core political speech could be blocked by a category that a library might use to comply with CIPA.

Moreover, there is evidence that other blocking software routinely denies access to gay and lesbian sites that contain core political speech. To take an example, N2H2, seller of a popular blocking product called Bess, has blocked a number of sites having to do with gay and lesbian issues under the category "Sex." These include sites dedicated to the problem of harassment of gays (http://www.inform.umd.edu/EdRes/Topic/Diversity/Specific/Sexual_Orientation/Reading/News/harassment); gay relationships (http://content.gay.com/channels/relationships); and the *Queer as Folk* television show (http://www.sho.com/queer). By discriminating in this manner against certain viewpoints, the secret criteria used in blocking software "may result in hidden censorship."

Nor is the risk of viewpoint discrimination confined to the software companies. There is also a danger that libraries could use the "technology protection measure" requirement as cover for viewpoint discrimination. Because CIPA does not place any limits on what type of blocking software a library may use, a librarian who was somehow aware of a systematic bias in a given blocking product could select software that discriminates against certain viewpoints based upon his or her own private agenda. Moreover, because the blocking software companies do not disclose the criteria that they use, the public would have little way of learning what had been done. Thus, commercial blocking software creates the danger of purposeful as well as unwitting viewpoint discrimination by libraries.

CIPA's "Technology Protection Measure" Requirement Should Be Subject to Strict Scrutiny

Th[e Supreme] Court has long recognized that certain methods of regulating speech pose a special danger to free speech and should therefore be subject to special scrutiny. Congress's attempt in CIPA to regulate speech by effectively forcing libraries to use technology produced by the market poses a similar danger and should therefore be subject to strict scrutiny.

The developers of blocking software enjoy unfettered discretion to select speech for suppression.

Few propositions are more deeply ingrained in constitutional law than the proposition that one particularly dangerous method of regulating speech—prior restraint—is subject to special scrutiny. . . . As th[e Supreme] Court has explained, a state is "not free to adopt whatever procedures it pleases for dealing with obscenity" because "[t]he administration of a censorship system . . . presents peculiar dangers to constitutionally protected speech." It is therefore well settled that "[a]ny system of prior restraints of expression comes . . . bearing a heavy presumption against its constitutional validity."

For example, licensing provisions that require prior approval of speech have long been recognized as "prior restraint[s] on speech" and are therefore subject to careful scrutiny, particularly where specific standards are lacking to guide the official doing the licensing. Th[e Supreme] Court has also considered other forms of regulation permitting public officials to review speech prior to its distribution to the public to be forms of censorship that should be treated as prior restraints and subjected to special scrutiny. . . . Moreover, in so doing, the Court has looked to the real-world effects of regulatory schemes to determine whether they act, as a practical matter, as prior restraints. . . .

CIPA's requirement that libraries wishing to make broad Internet access available to their patrons employ a commercially developed "technology protection measure" poses at least as great a risk of "freewheeling censorship," as previously recognized prior restraints. Like pre-publication censorship, blocking software reviews speech for its propriety, and like the local officials granted licensing authority in [previous court cases], the developers of blocking software enjoy unfettered discretion to select speech for suppression. Indeed, commercial blocking software is even more troubling because it effectively delegates censorship decisions to private individuals, who, unlike mayors, police officers, censor boards, and other public officials entrusted with issuing licenses, have no obligation to uphold the Constitution or narrowly tailor their censorship to comply with the First Amendment. To the contrary, as demonstrated above, blocking-software vendors may have powerful economic incentives to err on the side of suppressing more speech rather than less. The efforts of private software developers therefore deserve none of the deference traditionally due the efforts of the legislature or other public officials. Moreover, unlike licensing schemes that provide for judicial review of decisions to block speech, the use of blocking software proceeds without any "judicial determination." Thus, if any technique for regulating speech deserves judicial suspicion, it is CIPA's "technology protection measure."

Virtual Child Pornography Should Not Be Banned

Ambika J. Biggs

Ambika J. Biggs has been an intern at the First Amendment Center and a law student at the University of Virginia.

Groups working to stop child abduction and abuse hailed the PROTECT Act when President [George W.] Bush signed it into law [on] April 30, 2003. Aimed at protecting children from kidnappers and pedophiles, the Prosecutorial Remedies and Other Tools to end the Exploitation of Children Today Act created a national network to broadcast child abductions. It also targeted child pornographers, and toughened penalties for sexual abuse and kidnapping. Despite its worthy purposes, however, the law also included significant First Amendment implications that received little notice in press coverage.

These requirements affecting First Amendment rights were enacted in response to *Ashcroft v. Free Speech Coalition*, the 2002 Supreme Court decision that struck down key portions of the Child Pornography Prevention Act of 1996. After that ruling, several legislators scrambled to draft bills addressing child pornography. Sen. Orrin Hatch, R-Utah, was the chief sponsor of S. 151, the bill that eventually became the PROTECT Act.

The bill (sometimes called the "Amber Alert bill") also created a national rapid-response network to broadcast Amber Alerts—bulletins informing communities of kidnappings. The issue was of particular concern to Hatch because Elizabeth Smart, the 15-year-old who gained national attention when she was kidnapped [in 2002], is from Utah. Nine other sena-

Ambika J. Biggs, "The PROTECT Act and First Amendment," *First Amendment Center*, August 27, 2003. Reproduced by permission.

tors co-sponsored S. 151: Robert F. Bennett, R-Utah; John Edwards, D-N.C.; Patrick Leahy, D-Vt.; Mark Lunsford Pryor, D-Ark.; Richard Shelby, R-Ala.; Michael DeWine, R-Ohio; Charles E. Grassley, R-Iowa; Blanche Lincoln, D-Ark., and Charles E. Schumer, D-N.Y.

The *Free Speech Coalition* ruling "greatly weakened the laws pertaining to child pornography and left some gaping holes in our nation's ability to effectively prosecute child pornography offenses," Hatch said in a floor statement in January 2003. "We must now act quickly to repair our child pornography laws to provide for effective law enforcement in a manner that accords with the Court's ruling."

In a Jan. 29, 2003, letter to senators, the American Civil Liberties Union warned that certain provisions in S. 151 would prohibit or chill speech that the First Amendment protects. Nonetheless, several of those provisions became law, including ones that punish the possession and distribution of virtual child pornography; the distribution and advertisement of material that conveys the impression that it contains a depiction of a child engaging in sexually explicit conduct, regardless of whether it does; and the use of misleading Web-site names with the intent to trick people into viewing material that is obscene or harmful to minors.

The PROTECT Act passed 98-0 in the Senate and 400-25 in the House. Those margins aside, the First Amendment problems in the new law eventually may be matters for the courts to decide.

Prohibition on Virtual Child Pornography

Advocates of the PROTECT Act's new restrictions contend that some pedophiles show pornographic pictures to children in order to desensitize them and encourage them to engage in sexually explicit conduct. Targeting this practice, a section of Title V of the PROTECT Act bans virtual child pornography, which it describes as a "digital image, computer image, or computer-generated image that is, or is indistinguishable from, that of a minor engaging in sexually explicit conduct." Such a ban raises constitutional concerns.

[The Court ruled that] virtual child pornography is not 'intrinsically related' to the sexual abuse of children.

In *Free Speech Coalition*, the Court reaffirmed the illegality of pornography in which an actual child appears, but said virtual pornography in which no real children were used could be legal. It struck down the CPPA's prohibition of material that "appears to be of a minor engaging in sexually explicit conduct," as well as a ban on sexually explicit material distributed in such a way that it "conveys the impression" that it depicts a minor engaging in sexually explicit conduct. In other words, the *Free Speech Coalition* Court gave constitutional legitimacy to non-obscene creations of computer-generated pornography in which no real children are used. It distinguished real-child pornography from virtual child pornography by noting that children are harmed in the former, but not in the latter. The Court did not address the ban on morphing innocent pictures of real children into pictures in which they appear to be engaged in sexual activity; the defendants had not challenged that provision.

In *New York v. Ferber* (1982), the Court upheld a prohibition on the production, sale and distribution of child pornography because it was "intrinsically related" to the sexual abuse of children. Production not only harmed the children involved by serving as a record of their abuse, the Court said, but the sale or distribution of such pornography also economically motivated further production.

In contrast, "virtual child pornography is not 'intrinsically related' to the sexual abuse of children," the Court noted in *Free Speech Coalition*. The Court was not convinced by claims that the images can cause the sexual abuse of children. "The causal link is contingent and indirect," Justice Anthony Kennedy wrote for the majority. "The harm does not necessarily follow from the speech, but depends upon some unquantified potential for subsequent criminal acts." The ban on virtual child pornography "prohibits speech that records no crime and creates no victims by its production."

Furthermore, the Court said that even if some pedophiles use virtual child pornography to encourage children to participate in the acts, virtual child depictions could not be banned because many innocent things, such as candy and video games, also could be used for immoral purposes but would not be banned. Such a prohibition on virtual child depictions would "[run] afoul of the principle that speech within the rights of adults to hear may not be silenced completely in an attempt to shield children from it."

> *The First Amendment overbreadth doctrine prevents the government from banning or chilling a substantial amount of protected speech in an attempt to ban unprotected speech.*

Proponents of the CPPA say that the rise of virtual child pornography has created a problem for law enforcement agents, who often cannot distinguish between it and actual child pornography. "Technology has advanced so far that even experts often cannot say with absolute certainty that an image is real or a 'virtual' computer creation," Sen. Hatch said in introducing S. 151 in January 2003. According to the findings section of the act, since the Court struck down the CPPA, defendants in such cases "have almost universally raised the contention" that the materials police officers confiscated from them may not be real-child pornography, but rather virtual images.

Although the "solution" of banning both actual and virtual child pornography was not acceptable to the Supreme

Court in the *Free Speech Coalition* case, the PROTECT Act nonetheless calls for the same kind of ban. The findings section of the PROTECT Act notes that the Supreme Court decided *Ferber* more than 20 years ago, when the technology did not exist to create virtual images that are indistinguishable from real ones. The act's drafters decided to change the law to address this new technological capability. However, the First Amendment overbreadth doctrine prevents the government from banning or chilling a substantial amount of protected speech in an attempt to ban unprotected speech.

As the Court said in *Free Speech Coalition*, "The Government may not suppress lawful speech as a means to suppress unlawful speech. Protected speech does not become unprotected merely because it resembles the latter." The PROTECT Act bans images that are merely *indistinguishable* from a minor engaging in sexually explicit conduct. Under the act, "indistinguishable" means "an ordinary person viewing the depiction would conclude that the depiction is of an actual minor engaged in sexually explicit conduct." Such a ban could prohibit non-obscene computer-generated depictions that did not involve the use of any individuals and pornography created by using youthful-looking actors. Both kinds of expression are protected speech.

The PROTECT Act's proponents argue that it provides individuals wrongly accused of producing, possessing or selling child pornography with the opportunity to clear their names by demonstrating that actual minors were not used in the production. Notably, this affirmative defense shifts the burden from the accuser to the accused—dismissing the principle of "innocent until proven guilty." It also raises a feasibility problem. If law enforcement agents have a hard time finding those depicted in the images to prove they are under-age, then an individual accused only of possession of such images also may be unable to find the actors to prove they are of legal age. For those who claim to have created the pictures solely through computer imaging, the affirmative defense provides nearly no help—it would force them to prove a negative, that no real child was used in the creation of the pictures.

Prohibition on Falsely Advertising Child Pornography

Another section of Title V of the PROTECT Act prohibits knowingly advertising, promoting, presenting, distributing or soliciting "through the mails, or in interstate or foreign commerce by any means, including by computer, any material or purported material in a manner that reflects the belief, or that is intended to cause another to believe, that the material or purported material is, or contains (i) an obscene visual depiction of a minor engaging in sexually explicit conduct; or (ii) a visual depiction of an actual minor engaging in sexually explicit conduct." Here again, the Supreme Court did not look favorably on a similar provision in its *Free Speech Coalition* ruling.

In that case, the Court struck down as constitutionally overbroad a section of the CPPA that prohibited sexually explicit materials that "convey the impression" that they depict minors. The Court said the provision would ban films that did not contain child pornography but were advertised as such, and punish those who possessed the films knowing they had been mislabeled. The PROTECT Act may fail a constitutional challenge for similar reasons. The ACLU noted that problems arising out of false advertising and fraud could be addressed by the Federal Trade Commission.

Prohibition on Misleading Domain Names

Title V, Subtitle B of the PROTECT Act makes it illegal to use misleading domain names on the Internet with the intent to trick people into viewing obscenity. Free-speech advocates claim the "Truth in Domain Names" section is not constitutionally precise. "The term 'misleading' is inherently vague, which tends to chill protected speech on the Internet," the ACLU wrote to Sen. Hatch and Rep. James Sensenbrenner, R-Wis., on April 8, 2003. The act calls for fines or imprisonment for up to two years for those who use a misleading domain name intending to trick a person into viewing obscene material, and fines and up to four years' imprisonment for those who use the domain names to deceive a minor into viewing material that is harmful to minors.

Rep. Mike Pence, R-Ind., was among House members who crafted anti-pornography bills after the Supreme Court's ruling in *Free Speech Coalition*. His bill targeted pedophiles who trick children into viewing sexually explicit material by posting it on sites that have domain names that attract children, such as ones named after movies and toys. Language similar to that which he suggested made it into the PROTECT Act. He proposed that domain names that included the word "sex" to indicate the sexual content of the site would not be deemed misleading; the act expands the rule so that domain names that include the word "porn" also are not deemed misleading.

Though these provisions narrow the field of sites that would be deemed misleading, the provision still could be considered vague. For example, would domain names that don't contain these words but that have other words that suggest their pornographic content be considered misleading? "If the law is not precise, it may violate the First Amendment," the founder of Gigalaw.com, Doug Isenberg, wrote in a May 15, 2003, article on CNET News.com. In addition, domain owners are forced to incorporate certain words into their sites' domain names, which is a form of compelled speech, according to the ACLU. It also notes that such a provision makes it easier for individuals, including children, to find sexually explicit material on the Internet.

Prohibition on Sexual Expression That Is Not Obscene

The PROTECT Act also may raise constitutional issues because it prohibits sexual expression that is not necessarily obscene. The Supreme Court reaffirmed in *Free Speech Coalition* that the criteria established in *Miller v. California* (1973) still apply. Ordinarily the government can ban sexual expression only if it is obscene, but it can ban actual sexual depictions of children even if they're not obscene because the government has an interest in protecting children. Under the *Miller* test, material is obscene if:

- The average person, applying contemporary community standards, would find that the work, taken as a whole, appeals to the prurient interest.

- The work depicts or describes, in a patently offensive way, sexual conduct specifically defined by the applicable state law.

- The work, taken as a whole, lacks serious literary, artistic, political or scientific value.

Although the government clearly can ban all real-child pornography, it can only ban obscene virtual child pornography. The PROTECT Act bans virtual child pornography without considering whether it appeals to the prurient interest or is patently offensive, which could make it susceptible to a First Amendment challenge. The CPPA suffered from a similar problem, as the Court made clear in *Free Speech Coalition*. For example, under the CPPA and the PROTECT Act, pictures in psychology books and movies about sexual abuse could be prohibited, as could such popular movies as the 1996 *Romeo + Juliet* and the 1999 *American Beauty*.

Sexual abuse and exploitation of children is a serious matter. It stirs emotions and impassions people to take action to stop such terrible crimes. Legislators understandably struggle to create tough laws. In their haste, they may overlook and infringe on free-speech rights. The Supreme Court's ruling in *Free Speech Coalition*, however, serves as a warning that First Amendment rights must be protected, even when legislators are trying to solve a pressing problem.

Parents Should Be Responsible for Monitoring Their Children's Television Viewing

Adam Thierer

Adam Thierer was formerly the Cato Institute's director of tele-communications studies. He is now the director of the Center for Digital Media Freedom at the Progress & Freedom Foundation.

One of my earliest memories involves watching a monster movie on TV. I seem to recall it involved zombies hiding in a closet and grabbing people as they entered the room. Pretty creepy stuff and, quite honestly, I probably should not have been watching it. I'm not sure what mom was doing at the time, but she probably should have turned the TV off or found something better for me to watch.

If we are to believe some members of Congress, however, exposure to such violent images should have turned me into a madman. But even though I went on to watch more violent movies and programs, last time I checked, I still hadn't harmed or killed anyone. Like millions of other kids who grew up watching cowboy shoot-em-ups, weekend "creature features," or just plain old cops-and-robbers crime dramas, I learned how to separate fantasy from reality. Are there some unstable kids out there who are negatively influenced by violent images on TV? Sure. But one wonders how big that population really is and whether the root cause of their problems lies elsewhere (bad homes, bad neighborhoods, or even serious mental conditions). The academic literature is all over the place on this question and debates still rage about correlation versus causation when it comes to violent programming and aggressive behavior.

The Current Censorship Crusade

Regardless, our knights in shining armor in Congress are once again proposing to ride to our collective rescue and sanitize television "for the sake of the children." The "for the children" mantra has quickly become the universal pretext for legislative attempts to censor TV, radio, cable, video games and the Internet. Apparently, if you have the best interests of children in mind, you can dispense with the First Amendment and let the government censor whatever it pleases.

Maybe I sound like a broken record for posing this question in every essay on censorship I pen, but I'm going to go ahead and ask it again: What ever happened to personal and parental responsibility in this country? The responses I get generally fall into one of two camps. One group says personal responsibility died a slow but certain death in this country a long time ago and that I'm just another principled but quixotic dreamer who has yet to come to grips with the inevitability of government censorship. This group doesn't like the sound of censorship, but is apparently willing to live with it, or they've just given up fighting the good fight. Another group, however, openly embraces the idea of Uncle Sam playing the role of surrogate parent in our homes. They lament the fact that media is so ubiquitous in our lives today and say they've largely given up trying to keep tabs on what their kids watch or listen to.

Either way, a lot of people appear ready to raise the white flag and let government censor "for the children." So the censorship crusade *du jour*, aimed at getting "excessive violence" out of the media, suddenly seems like a very real possibility. The Senate included a measure in a military spending bill (how's that for irony!) that would ban violent video programming on broadcast TV during hours in which children might be in the audience (basically anytime before 10:00 p.m.). And 39 members of the House Commerce Committee recently wrote the FCC [Federal Communications Commission] requesting that the agency study what it could do about violence on television. The FCC quickly responded by announcing a new inquiry into the issue. Meanwhile, there are still lurking threats of regulation of supposedly overly violent video games at both the federal and state levels.

Flaws of Government Censorship

But while the censorship bandwagon is really rolling . . . in the wake of the Janet Jackson incident I would hope there are a few brave souls left out there willing to fight attempts by Beltway [Washington, D.C.] bureaucrats to dictate what our families can see or hear. The fundamental problem with proposals to censor violence in media is that they will require that the government make myriad "eye of the beholder" decisions about what is "too violent" on behalf of *all* Americans. Choices that we should be making voluntarily for ourselves and our children are suddenly choices made through the political process, with its coercive ability to silence any views or content it finds unacceptable.

Parents need to act responsibly and exercise their private right—indeed, responsibility—to censor their children's eyes and ears from certain things.

Consider the ramifications of allowing a handful of folks down at the FCC to determine what constitutes "excessive violence." Are the bloody and occasionally gruesome scenes in *CSI* and *ER* excessive, or is that a reasonable depiction of forensic and medical science? Hockey games on prime-time TV feature lots of fights, blood, and lost teeth. For decades, cartoons have offered a buffet of violent acts, and slapstick comedy of the Three Stooges variety features a lot of unforgivingly violent moments presented as humor. Should regulators also censor the many combat-oriented video games on the market today that involve extremely realistic military training and war game scenarios, some of which even rely on the consulting services of former military officials? How about gruesome war scenes from actual combat that any child can see on the nightly news? What about the stabbing, poisoning, and other heinous acts found in Shakespeare's tragedies? And, for God's sake (excuse the pun), what about all the violence in the Bible or Mel Gibson's *The Passion of the Christ*?

Parents' Responsibility

I could go on and on, but you get the point. This all comes down to a question of who calls the shots—parents or government—regarding what we are allowed to see and hear in a free society. This is not to say society must celebrate or even defend violence in the media; there are plenty of movies, shows and games that do contain what many parents would regard as a troubling amount of violent content for young children to witness. Parents need to act responsibly and exercise their private right—indeed, responsibility—to censor their children's eyes and ears from certain things. It's become increasingly evident, however, that a lot of parents have just gotten lazy about carrying out this difficult job. While I can appreciate the hassle of constantly trying to monitor a child's viewing and listening habits, that's no excuse for throwing in the towel and calling in the government to censor what the rest of the world has access to.

By the way, let's not forget that we long ago opened the door to government censorship when we allowed them to mandate that those silly "V-Chips" be installed in every TV set to supposedly help us censor sex and violence. Have you ever met anyone who uses them? Neither have I, but many lawmakers will use that fact as yet another reason to censor more directly. Those who were ridiculed for predicting that the V-Chip could lead to more far-reaching censorship of violence on television deserve an apology.

Finally, one wonders what all this hand-wringing over violence means for cable and satellite programs and providers. This has been a watershed year in terms of congressional attempts to assert control over content on pay TV, with several proposals flying to "do something" about indecency on cable. And now the Senate wants to regulate violence on cable too, although it is willing to carve out "premium" or pay-per-view services. Thus, *The Sopranos* gets a pass while *Nip/Tuck* and *The Shield* are apparently fair game for the censors. All because the Senate argues that "broadcast television, cable television and video programming are uniquely pervasive presences in the lives of all American children, and (are) readily accessible to all American children." Again, it's all "for the children." But is there anyone left in government who will stand up for freedom, the First Amendment, and personal responsibility?

CHAPTER 4

Should Speech That Endangers National Security Be Censored?

Chapter Preface

On December 16, 2005, the *New York Times* published an explosive story alleging that the federal government was spying on people inside the United States without first getting a search warrant. The government claimed that this "warrantless wiretapping," as it came to be called, was legal and was necessary to help catch terrorists. Some government officials and legal scholars disagreed, arguing that the program was unconstitutional.

The *New York Times* admitted that the government had asked them not to publish the story, and said that they had waited a year after first hearing about the program to run the article. The *Times* also claimed that they had left out some information that the government thought could aid terrorists. Still, the story left some of the people who read it appalled that the *New York Times* would potentially compromise national security by printing details of an anti-terrorism operation.

This was not the first time that the *New York Times* had caused a controversy by publishing government secrets. During the Vietnam War the newspaper's case for the right to print classified information that it had acquired was heard by the Supreme Court. That case, *New York Times Co. v. United States*, began when a former Department of Defense employee copied large parts of a classified report on the conduct of the Vietnam War and gave the copies to the *New York Times*. This employee, Daniel Ellsberg, believed that the American public had been lied to about the Vietnam War and that they deserved to know the truth. The *Times* began publishing the documents, which became known as the "Pentagon Papers," on June 13, 1971. The Justice Department sued the *Times* and convinced a judge to temporarily order the *Times* to halt the publication.

Due to the importance of the case the appeals process was drastically sped up, allowing the case to reach the Supreme Court less than two weeks after the first portion of the papers was published. The Supreme Court ruled that the government could not legally forbid newspapers from publishing this information. "Only a free and unrestrained press can effectively expose deception in government," Justice Hugo Black wrote in his opinion. "To find that the President has 'inherent power' to halt the publication of news by resort to the courts would wipe out the First Amendment."

This decision was controversial at the time, and the principle that the press cannot be forbidden from publishing information that could harm national security remains controversial today. In the following chapter, the authors debate how much power the government should have to restrict speech in order to protect national security.

The Press Should Not Publish Leaked Classified Material

Pat Buchanan

Pat Buchanan is an author and syndicated columnist and was the Reform Party's 2000 presidential candidate.

Mary McCarthy, special assistant to President [Bill] Clinton and senior director of intelligence in his White House, has been fired by the CIA [Central Intelligence Agency].

McCarthy allegedly told the *Washington Post* our NATO [North Atlantic Treaty Organization] allies were secretly letting the CIA operate bases on their soil for the interrogation of terror suspects. Apparently, McCarthy failed several polygraph tests, after which she confessed.

If true, she was faithless to her oath, betrayed the trust of her country, damaged America's ties to foreign intelligence agencies and governments, and broke the law. The Justice Department is investigating whether McCarthy violated the Espionage Act.

Journalists Praised While Sources Are Punished

Yet, while she may be headed for criminal prosecution and prison, the *Post* reporter to whom she leaked intelligence on the secret sites, Dana Priest, just won a Pulitzer Prize for revealing the existence of these sites.

Also copping Pulitzers were two reporters for the *New York Times* who revealed that, since 9-11, U.S. intelligence agencies have been intercepting calls and e-mails between terror suspects and U.S. citizens.

Pat Buchanan, "Of Pulitzers and Treason," Townhall.com, April 25, 2006. Reproduced by permission.

President [George W.] Bush had implored the *Times* not to publish the story, lest exposure of the spying program alert [terrorist group] al-Qaida to U.S. capabilities and operations.

For one year, the *Times* held the story—then, it went with it. While the delay has been criticized by some journalists, most applauded exposing the spying program and the U.S. secret bases, and the Pulitzers that went with their exposure.

On ABC's *This Week*, Sen. John Kerry, to whose campaign McCarthy made a $2,000 contribution, was his usual ambivalent self when asked whether he approved of what she had done:

"Of course not. A CIA agent has the obligation to uphold the law, and clearly leaking is against the law, and nobody should leak. I don't like leaking. But if you're leaking to tell the truth, Americans are going to look at that, at least mitigate or think about what are the consequences that you . . . put on that person. Obviously they're not going to keep their job, but there are other larger issues here."

What "larger issues" there were, Kerry did not say.

Pressed by ABC's George Stephanopoulos, Kerry blurted, "I'm glad she told the truth, but she's going to obviously—if she did it, if she did it—suffer the consequences of breaking the law."

Kerry was prepared for the question, so he has to be held to account. When he says, "I'm glad she told the truth," one has to ask: What is Kerry talking about?

To whom did McCarthy tell the truth? Apparently, to Dana Priest, in exposing the secret program. Is Kerry "glad" she did this? Is he glad she violated her oath and broke the law and exposed the program? To those to whom McCarthy owed loyalty, her superiors at the CIA, she apparently lied in her polygraph examinations, and only after being caught did she confess.

Where is the moral heroism in clandestinely violating one's oath, breaking the law, leaking secrets and lying about it? Is this the New Morality? What was the higher cause McCarthy was serving?

Journalists Are Not Above the Law

Journalists are rising to her defense, describing McCarthy as a whistle-blower—i.e., someone who calls the government to account for wrongdoing. But there is no evidence President Bush or U.S. agencies were doing anything criminal by using secret sites provided by NATO allies to interrogate terror suspects plotting to murder Americans.

If U.S. officials are engaged in misconduct or atrocities at these bases—i.e., the torture of prisoners—no one has said so. Reportedly, an E.U. [European Union] investigation of the U.S. secret sites in Europe turned up nothing.

What does it say about American journalism that it gives its most prestigious prizes to reporters who acquire and reveal illicitly leaked U.S. secrets, when the result is to damage the U.S. government in a time of war? Both the *Times* and *Post* got their Pulitzers for fencing secrets of the U.S. government, criminally leaked by disloyal public servants they continue to protect.

What does it say about American journalism that it gives its most prestigious prizes to reporters who acquire and reveal illicitly leaked U.S. secrets?

Query: If McCarthy deserves firing, disgrace and possibly prison for what she did, does the *Post* deserve congratulations for collaborating with and covering up her infidelity, deceit and possible criminality?

Are journalists above the law? Are they entitled to publish secrets, the leaking of which can put their sources in jail for imperiling the national security? What kind of business has journalism become . . . ?

[Former vice presidential chief of staff] Scooter Libby is to be tried for perjury for allegedly lying to a grand jury investigating whether he leaked the name of CIA operative Valerie Plame, in a White House campaign to discredit war critic Joe

Wilson. Larry Franklin of the Pentagon got 12 years for leaking military secrets to the Israeli lobby.

McCarthy deserves the same treatment. She should be prosecuted and, if convicted, spend the next decade in prison. Whether this war was a mistake or not, no one has the right to sabotage the war effort.

Not even journalists.

Supporters of Anti-American Terrorism Should Be Barred from Entering the United States

Steve Emerson

Steve Emerson is the executive director of the Investigative Project on Terrorism.

No case illustrates the murderous deception of Western society by Islamic militants more than the recent episode involving Tariq Ramadan, the Swiss professor who was denied a visa to teach at Notre Dame. His supporters in the U.S. rallied vigorously around Ramadan, protesting with total moral certitude the politically outrageous move by the U.S. government to muzzle a Muslim "moderate." The coalition to defend Ramadan included the *New York Times*, the *Washington Post*, academic boards around the country, Islamic advocacy groups and human-rights groups. Their near unanimous message was that Ramadan was a genuine "moderate" and "Islamic pluralist," but that even if one disagreed with some of his statements, Ramadan surely should have been entitled to have his ideas debated in the great free marketplace of ideas of the American campus.

Miraculously, the coalition of high priests of political correctness, [conservative Muslim] Wahhabi groups masquerading as pluralists, and the elite censors of fair and balanced journalism did not prevail. Ramadan was not given a visa and soon, in an act of righteous indignation, refused to reapply for another visa.

Steven Emerson, "Islam's Grand Wizard of Deception," *WorldNetDaily*, April 2, 2005. © 2005 WorldNetDaily.com, Inc. Reproduced by permission.

Deception by Radical Islamic Groups

Even after the murderous actions by Islamic militants on 9-11 in the U.S. and their carrying out or planning terrorist operations in more than 90 countries between 1990 and 2003, the American intelligentsia, in a devilish collusion with radical Islamic groups hiding under false veneer, have managed to perpetrate the grand deception of militant Islam: pretending to be moderate (small d) democrats, pluralists and victims of hate.

Radical Islamic groups have continued to invert reality, turning facts on their head, in a stunning ability to anoint themselves as the victims of hate as opposed to the murderous reality that they are the progenitors of hate. Where else could radical Islamic leaders like Yousef Al Qardawi, a leader of the Muslim Brotherhood who calls for killing Jews (not just Israelis but Jews) and Americans (not just occupiers), be described as "moderate" or a pro-Western "reformer" or variations of this theme (*Washington Post, New York Times, Christian Science Monitor, Los Angeles Times*)?

Where else could one hear that jihad [holy war] was a "beautiful" concept, as was broadcast recently on National Public Radio [NPR], devoid of any violent or militant meaning? NPR's commentator was the daughter of an Islamic American leader who justified the killing of Robert Kennedy—a fact NPR withheld from its listeners but paled in comparison to its brazen willingness to air a *de facto* commercial for al-Qaida—with the commentator ending her Islamist (taxpayer-subsidized) infomercial with the following line: "Someday, I hope 'jihad' will find its way back into our lexicon, when it can be used properly, in sentences like 'She's on a jihad to achieve the American Dream.'"

In the decade and a half before 9-11, Hamas, Islamic Jihad, al-Qaida and virtually every other radical Islamic group and leader successfully perpetrated the most brilliant strategic enemy deception in U.S. history by planting themselves in the heart of enemy territory under false cover as nonprofit (and of course tax-deductible) humanitarian groups, civil-rights groups and non-political religious institutions. Until 9-11, the deceit had continued with staggering success as radical Islamic groups and leaders were routinely invited to the White House, provided with federal funding, praised by politicians and lionized by the media.

But before this charade was exposed, nearly 3,000 Americans were forced to pay with their lives as the price for the belated realization that we had been had. Suddenly, charities that had been secretly operating as conduits for terrorists and established American Muslim leaders leading double lives as terrorist masterminds were finally being recognized for what they were: terrorists. And instead of being toasted at the State Department, they were now more appropriately being prosecuted, shut down and deported.

Ramadan has repeatedly provided a justification for terrorist acts against U.S. allies such as Israel and Russia and . . . against the U.S. itself.

And yet, more than three years after 9-11, it would seem that this same homicidal self-delusion is alive and well in the United States. This is where Ramadan comes to play such a pivotal role in highlighting the danger of this continued self-deception.

Statements by Ramadan

First, Ramadan is not any more a moderate than [former Ku Klux Klan leader] David Duke would be considered a moderate on race relations. The only difference is that David Duke is not smart enough to speak in two languages, cloak his racism under the mantle of pluralism or enjoy the witting collaboration of the media.

In several interviews given to various European publications over the last few years, Ramadan has repeatedly provided a justification for terrorist acts against U.S. allies such as Israel and Russia and, more recently, against the U.S. itself. Asked by the Italian magazine *Panorama* if the killing of civilians is right, Ramadan unambiguously responded, "In Palestine, Iraq, Chechnya, there is a situation of oppression, repression and dictatorship. It is legitimate for Muslims to resist fascism that kills the innocent." When asked if car bombings against U.S. forces in Iraq were legitimate, professor Ramadan responded, "Iraq was colonized by the Americans. The resistance against the army is just."

Preachers like Tariq Ramadan 'can exert an influence on young Islamists and therefore constitute an incitement that can lead them to join violent groups.'

Mastering the art of *taqiyya* (double speaking to fool the unbelievers), Tariq Ramadan has enchanted many with his apparent moderation. But a careful examination of his words reveals that professor Ramadan is not what he seems and claims to be. Yes, he says that he "agrees with integration" of Muslims in the West, but he is careful to say that "we [Muslims] are the ones who are going to decide the content." He mollifies by saying that he accepts Western secular law, but—here's the catch—"only if this law doesn't force me to do things against my religion." And when he is cornered with questions on the brutality of some punishments of Islamic law, such as stoning, he tells us that he is against them, but (there is always a "but") they are in Quranic texts and so he cannot fully condemn them, and we have to settle for "an absolute moratorium on all physical punishments."

The telegenic, soft-spoken and charming professor is just the modern, Westernized face of the same enemy that wears a different mask on other battlefields. As the distinguished expert of Middle East affairs Fouad Ajami recently wrote, Tariq Ramadan is "in the world of the new Islamism, pure nobility." His moderate façade hides his radical heart, and just a careful read of his words would reveal it. France, the country that knows him best, has made up its mind on him. A court in Lyon recently said that preachers like Tariq Ramadan "can exert an influence on young Islamists and therefore constitute an incitement that can lead them to join violent groups."

In France at least, some leftist intellectuals have recognized Ramadan for what he is. The self-censorious *New York Times* was even forced to report that Bernard-Henri Levy, who wrote the best seller *Who Killed Daniel Pearl?*, accused Ramadan of being the "intellectual champion of all kinds of double-talk" with a "racist vision of the world" and having promoted anti-Semitism. The *Times* further reported that Bernard Kouchner, the foreign aid advocate and former health minister of France, called Ramadan "absolutely a kook with no historical memory" and "a dangerous man." He added, "The way he denounced some Jewish intellectuals is close to anti-Semitism."

Arguments Against Granting Ramadan a Visa

Still, the Ramadan fan club in the U.S. continued to portray the exclusion of Mr. Ramadan as part of an anti-Muslim campaign. The charge of anti-Muslim racism, part of the larger orchestration by radical Muslims to portray themselves as the victims of hate, has been mastered perfectly, requiring only the collaboration of the American media. At the height of the controversy [in 2004], the *New York Times* opined that "American Muslim groups questioned the government's ability or willingness to distinguish between what they see as Muslim moderates like Mr. Ramadan and extremists." But who were these American Muslim groups, portrayed by the *Times* as intellectually honest arbiters of who really is a moderate? None other than off-shoots and branches of the Muslim Brotherhood, the Islamic radical movement that gave birth to al-Qaida and Hamas, and whose founder was none other than Hassan Al-Banna, the grandfather of Ramadan.

And there are those who fall back on the free-market response: Is the most powerful nation in the world afraid of allowing Ramadan access to the intellectual pluralism of the U.S., where free speech is honored as the most sacred privilege that we have?

It is preposterous to ask the U.S. government . . . to grant this privilege [of entry into the United States] to a person who openly condones attacks against U.S. forces and interests.

Well, Ramadan does not need to be in the United States to convey his message and thoughts. Through the Internet, media and instant telecommunications, the American public is not being denied one iota of Ramadan's propaganda.

After the first World Trade Center bombing in 1993, the same defenders of Ramadan—the *New York Times* and other elite media—were the first to ask probing and indignant questions about how the Blind Sheik, with his radical views, was able to get visas to the United States in the early 1990s. But that was before he was indicted or convicted of any U.S. crime. So apparently, the high priests at the time decided that the premium of free speech for non-U.S. guests was not sacred; that in fact, the right to visit the U.S. was not a constitutional right afforded to any citizen of the world, a view unfortunately increasingly espoused by editorial boards.

Title 8 U.S. Code Section 1182 requires the exclusion from the U.S. of any alien who has "used his position of prominence within any country to endorse or espouse terrorist activity, or to persuade others to support terrorist activity or a terrorist organization." The provision seems written to fit Ramadan's case. The entry into the United States of any foreign national is, by law, a privilege and not a right. It is pre- posterous to ask the U.S. government to disregard its own laws and to grant this privilege to a person who openly con- dones attacks against U.S. forces and interests.

Aside from the legal justification for barring Ramadan, the moral reason for keeping him out is the same reason the U.S. has for years denied visas to neo-Nazi proponents from West- ern Europe. It is not only the access to the United States that both neo-Nazis and Ramadan have sought. Rather it is the of- ficial imprimatur of the U.S. government, an effective declara- tion of political legitimacy attending to the granting of the visa. And that is precisely the same legitimacy that allowed militant Islamic groups to operate for so long in the United States. Do we really want to repeat history?

Scientific Information That Could Help Terrorists Should Be Restricted

Mitchel B. Wallerstein

Mitchel B. Wallerstein is the dean of Syracuse University's Maxwell School of Citizenship and Public Affairs.

I have been concerned professionally for more than two decades with the relationship between scientific openness and national security. Indeed, just more than twenty years ago, I had the privilege of directing a National Academy of Sciences panel that issued a report entitled *Scientific Communication and National Security*, known informally as the Corson Report, after Dale Corson, the panel's chair and president emeritus of Cornell University. Thus, for me, today's discussions about science and security have, in the immortal words of [renowned baseball player] Yogi Berra, a strong sense of "déjà vu all over again."

The nature of the threat has changed, of course, since the Corson panel issued its report. The target of restrictions on open communication of scientific information is no longer the former Soviet Union and Warsaw Treaty states. But the risks to scientific and technological progress and the potential negative effects of imposing restrictions remain similar.

After working on the Corson Report and related studies at the National Academy in the 1980s, I managed major aspects of the U.S. Department of Defense's policy on technology security and export controls from 1993 to 1997. Even though my time in government preceded the terrible events of September 11, 2001, I can report that we recognized during the 1990s that certain areas of science, such as biotechnology,

Mitchel B. Wallerstein, "After the Cold War: A New Calculus for Science and Security," *Academe*, September–October 2003. Reproduced by permission of the author.

could be enormously helpful to the so-called proliferant states, such as Iraq and North Korea, as well as to terrorist groups seeking to gain access to mass-casualty weapons—or weapons of mass destruction. (Proliferant states are states known to possess, or strongly suspected of seeking to acquire or develop, nuclear, chemical, or biological weapons and their means of delivery.)

I had forgotten, until I went back recently to review the Corson Report, that the panel had anticipated the need to consider how restrictions on scientific communication would differ in an era in which the principal security threats did not emanate from the Soviet Union and Warsaw Treaty states. This observation was, however, simply noted toward the end of the report as a subject that the National Academy might wish to address in the future.

Scientific Espionage in Soviet Times

Of course, the fact that the threats we worry about today no longer derive from a monolithic adversary with considerable science and technology capabilities necessarily must alter the calculus of how we think about the problem. During the era of the Soviet Union, we faced an opponent that, because of the shortcomings of its science and technology infrastructure and its economic constraints, undertook a systematic and sustained effort to obtain scientific and technological information from the West. It did so by taking advantage of the openness of the western science and technology community. It sent agents to scientific meetings to search for specific information (or someone who could be co-opted to supply it); it placed supposed "students" onto university campuses where they could gain access to leading-edge research; and it engaged in many other activities, both overt and covert. These efforts were well documented by the intelligence community, and some were fairly successful.

In 1981, in response to this growing threat, senior officials in the incoming [Ronald] Reagan administration began to call—loudly at times—for compartmentalizing sensitive research on university campuses and in the private sector and for excluding many foreign nationals from participation in such research. This development alarmed the leadership of the science and technology community, including university presidents. Shortly thereafter, the National Academy presidents set up the panel on scientific communication and national security that issued the Corson Report.

It was (and is) not individual widgets or weapons component technology that must be protected, but the knowledge base and technical know-how necessary to design and build them.

I dwell on this history to make a point: in the Soviet era, we had a technically sophisticated adversary that, if it succeeded in gaining access to sensitive research and analysis, would have been able to overcome the gap in fielded weapons systems between itself and nations of the North Atlantic Treaty Organization. This gap gave the West its technological dominance, which, in turn, maintained the strategic parity between the opposing sides in the Cold War despite the substantial numerical superiority of the Warsaw Treaty forces.

What the Corson Report pointed out, however, was that, with few exceptions, it was (and is) not individual widgets or weapons component technology that must be protected, but the knowledge base and technical know-how necessary to design and build them. This seemingly obvious but important observation applies to every major threat from weapons of mass destruction we face today, including that posed by nuclear, biological, and chemical weapons, and even more esoteric weapons such as those used in cyberwarfare.

Post–Cold War Concerns

The most immediate concern driving recent federal legislation and executive branch actions—including the enshrinement of the ambiguous term, "sensitive homeland security information"—is the fear that al Qaeda and other terrorist groups may gain access to the knowledge and materials necessary to build crude, but nevertheless deadly, mass-casualty weapons for use against the United States or its interests or citizens abroad.

But that is not the only reason to worry about unrestricted communication of sensitive science and technology information. Let me name two others: the so-called proliferant states (especially Iran, Iraq, and North Korea) and China. Credible evidence exists that some proliferant states continue to seek information (and people) in the West to help them develop indigenous nuclear weapons and other weapons of mass destruction. And China, which is, of course, already a nuclear weapons state, is modernizing its military and possibly expanding its force projection capabilities.

I would argue, however, that both of these threats more closely resemble the old concerns about the Soviet science and technology acquisition effort. We know how to deal with such threats, and the research management procedures now in place are generally adequate to cope with the problem. But the number of Chinese nationals working and studying today in the U.S. science and technology sector is large indeed, and their presence could become a matter of concern if political and military relations with China deteriorate later. . . .

The Terrorist Threat

The issue of terrorist acquisition of scientific information and know-how is of a different character from these other threats that have been with us, in one form or another, for the last quarter-century. As a general rule, terrorists do not need—nor, in all likelihood, can they readily make use of—massive volumes of basic scientific knowledge or advanced techniques.

In Soviet times, we worried about protecting the physics knowledge and engineering expertise needed to build smaller, faster computer chips, or the extraordinarily complex computer algorithms used to design the hot sections of high-bipass jet engines. Terrorists, however, are neither designing nor manufacturing weapons systems. They lack the economic resources, the personnel, and the physical infrastructure to accomplish this task.

The principal area in which the acquisition of technical know-how could directly and substantially benefit terrorist organizations and proliferant states is biological science.

What they are intent on—and apparently quite good at—is constructing (often in ingenious and unconventional ways) a small number of weapons of mass destruction, most often by acquiring details about their operational and design characteristics. But will further restrictions on the communication of scientific information or on the access by foreign students to the U.S. research system do anything significant to impede terrorist acquisition of weapons of mass destruction?

Biological Weapons

In my view, the principal area in which the acquisition of technical know-how could directly and substantially benefit terrorist organizations and proliferant states is biological science. Clearly, the communication of information that helps improve knowledge about dangerous pathogens, their effects, safe handling of them, and so on increases the chance that they can be made into weapons covertly on a small scale. It has been an informal rule of thumb since the Cold War that the narrower the gap between the acquisition of new scientific knowledge and efforts to embody that knowledge in technical applications, the greater the likelihood of the unintended transfer of potentially dangerous technology or technical expertise.

Biotechnology and biological warfare threats are of extraordinary concern for another reason as well: it does not require a huge investment in physical infrastructure or many highly trained researchers to achieve modest success. The experience of the Aum Shinrikyo cult in Japan is instructive. The Aum Shinrikyo was the first terrorist organization outside the United States (there was at least one inside as well) to attempt to acquire both chemical and biological weapons. After the arrest of the cult's leaders, which unfortunately did not occur until after a sarin [nerve] gas attack on the Tokyo subway in 1995, and after some less successful (and not as well publicized) efforts to develop biological weapons, the authorities found and explored the Aum Shinrikyo research and development facility near Mount Fuji.

What they found was shocking: the cult had recruited to its ranks a small number of chemical engineers and life scientists who were at work developing and testing chemical and biological weapons. (Investigators even discovered subsequently that the Aum Shinrikyo had rented an abandoned sheep station in western Australia to test the weapons it had developed.) The entire undertaking, including the acquisition of equipment, precursor chemicals and pathogens, and so on was financed by the sect. But the key to its success was the recruitment of a small cadre of individuals with sufficient technical training and knowledge.

Principles for Scientific Security

So what about the development of present-day principles for determining whether or not science and technology information should be kept (or made) secret for security reasons? Having observed and worked on the problem from within and outside the government, I have reached the following conclusions.

1. Rational and well-conceived restrictions do remain necessary, but they can and must be applied to substantially fewer areas of scientific inquiry and technology development than in Cold War days. No rationale remains for a large, overreaching list of controlled items and subject areas.

2. In fields such as biotechnology, the publication of what some would call the "recipes" for doing things at the laboratory bench level should be avoided in most cases. As the Corson panel noted, it is often difficult to transfer such know-how unless qualified scientists can gain hands-on experience at the bench level.

3. Unfettered access to scientific knowledge on university campuses remains as important today as it was twenty years ago. On this point, the Corson panel surely had it right, and the dependence of the U.S. research system on foreign students, postdoctoral researchers, and faculty has only grown in the interim. But that does not mean that we cannot devise ways to be more vigilant about who is permitted to gain entry to our country and to our research facilities. The September 11 hijackers "hid in plain sight" in our communities before carrying out their deadly violence. Thus, sad to say, universities and private research enterprises must devote greater effort to reviewing the backgrounds of foreign nationals whom they admit for graduate training or hire in their laboratories. And the government will need to work even more closely with the universities and the private sector in determining who should be granted a visa for study or work in the United States.

4. The areas of scientific knowledge and technological application that are immediately germane to the development of weapons of mass destruction are well known at this point. Because we are not dealing with an adversary that is capable of broadly vacuuming up knowledge or

expertise, advances in many—perhaps most—disciplinary areas can be discussed and communicated with little or minimal restrictions. Unfortunately, however, those areas or subdisciplines of the life sciences associated with the development of biological weapons must continue to be subject to a different set of rules. As the Corson panel and other more recent studies recommended, work in such areas may best be undertaken at off-campus facilities, where the matter of excluding foreigners, when necessary, is perhaps more manageable.

5. That said, the scientific enterprise depends on the rapid publication and dissemination (whether physical or virtual) of new results and ideas. As repeated studies have concluded, we will damage the very capability that has made us the world's leading techno-scientific power if we allow our new security concerns to impede this process. Nevertheless, a modest publication delay for purposes of security review may be appropriate in areas of the life sciences in which the rapid communication of research results may have direct application to the design of biological weapons, improve knowledge about handling dangerous pathogens, or help a terrorist organization or a proliferant state avoid costly dead-end lines of research or overcome other technical obstacles. For research not undertaken with federal funding, I can imagine such a review conducted voluntarily by a duly constituted body of the life sciences community.

6. Fortunately, terrorist organizations continue to have difficulty purchasing so-called enabling technology, such as sophisticated laboratory measurement equipment, containment devices, and the like. Nevertheless, the U.S. government and equipment manufacturers also must remain vigilant regarding the end-user(s) of transferred technology.

Before concluding, I want to comment briefly on two other aspects of the problem. First, there is the legitimate question of what the United States can realistically expect to accomplish on its own. To state the obvious, the U.S. research system is not the only place where important life sciences research is carried out that may be of interest to terrorists and the agents of proliferant states. The European Union, Japan, and other advanced states have research infrastructures equally capable of producing and disseminating such information. Thus, despite some highly regrettable unilateral actions taken by the U.S. government, limitations on the communication of sensitive science and technology information can work only if they are adopted multilaterally. This matter requires urgent attention, and perhaps an international meeting of experts.

Finally, since Cold War days, universities have, quite frankly, tried to have it both ways. They have sought large amounts of public funding to conduct basic and applied research while resisting periodic calls for the adoption of "codes of conduct" and other means to address concerns about how foreign nationals use the advanced training and knowledge they acquire in the United States when they return to their own countries. This apparent contradiction has continued to perplex me over the years. It would seem that today, more than ever, faculty, research staff, and administrators who manage work in sensitive research areas must be vigilant about the motivations and intentions of their students and co-workers. They should strive to impart a value structure that emphasizes the positive role of science and technology in advancing the interests and needs of humanity and guards against its use to cause mass casualties and human suffering.

Punishing Reporters of Leaked Classified Information Threatens the Practice of Journalism

Paul K. McMasters

Paul K. McMasters is the ombudsman of the First Amendment Center, a not-for-profit group that promotes First Amendment freedoms.

What if the practice of journalism became a crime?

Imagine the possibilities. Computer screens carrying news and commentary would blink and go blank. Wire-service bureaus would close up shop. TV news studio lights would sputter and go dark. With a heavy shudder, printing presses would grind to a stop.

Ah, blessed silence.

Ah, blissful ignorance.

Ah, shrugging off the shackles of freedom.

Such a flight of fancy is preposterous, of course. Yet we cannot dismiss the reality that for an increasing number of journalists, subpoenas, grand jury inquiries, court battles, huge legal bills and possibly jail cells could be the reward for doing well in their constitutional calling.

Threat to the Use of Anonymous Sources

Right now, more than 30 journalists in half a dozen different cases, criminal and civil, are confronted with subpoenas that will force them either to reveal their confidential sources or go to jail to protect them. These journalists didn't commit a

Paul K. McMasters, "Bad News for Good Journalism," *First Amendment Center*, March 26, 2006. Reproduced by permission.

crime. They did commit themselves to protecting the sources who helped them to bring to the nation's attention important information about threats to our freedom or risks to our safety: warrantless spying on American citizens, secret interrogation centers for terrorism suspects in foreign countries, the mishandling of nuclear secrets and investigations of anthrax poisonings and California Muslims suspected of ties to terrorists.

Many professionals within federal law enforcement agencies no doubt would prefer to devote their energies to fighting terrorism, crime and corruption than to expend additional resources tracking down whistleblowers and journalists. Many political leaders, on the other hand, have seemed more alarmed by leaks and news stories than by the policies and actions that have provoked them.

[In February 2006], CIA Director Porter Goss railed against leaks of sensitive information before a Senate committee and made no secret of his stance: "It is my aim and it is my hope that we will witness a grand jury investigation with reporters present being asked to reveal who is leaking this information."

Sen. Pat Roberts, R-Kan., chairman of the Senate intelligence committee, says he is interested in a law that bears a painful resemblance to Great Britain's Official Secrets Act, which allows for the prosecution and muzzling of journalists and citizens who receive sensitive information.

His counterpart in the House, Rep. Pete Hoekstra, R-Mich., is similarly predisposed toward such an exception to our free-speech freedoms.

Officials of the U.S. Justice Department are not waiting for legislative action. They apparently believe they can accomplish the same thing in the courts, Remarkably, a federal judge has encouraged their constitutional adventurism with an extraordinary ruling.

Threat to Reporting Based on Classified Information

On Jan. 20, Judge T.S. Ellis III sentenced Lawrence Franklin, a mid-level Pentagon analyst, to 12 and a half years in prison for providing classified information to two lobbyists. That was not so remarkable an outcome, except that Judge Ellis went further and endorsed the federal prosecutors' assertions that the recipients of that information also could be prosecuted.

"Persons who have unauthorized possession, who come into unauthorized possession of classified information, must abide by the law. That applies to academics, lawyers, journalists, professors, whatever," Judge Ellis said from the bench during his sentencing statement. The law he refers to is the Espionage Act of 1917.

Thus, what had been a somewhat obscure case is now making waves throughout the nation's capital and elsewhere as the two recipients of Franklin's information, Steve Rosen and Keith Weissman, former employees of the American Israel Public Affairs Committee, head to trial . . . before Judge Ellis.

Secrecy and security are not always the same thing.

If the judge follows his initial statement and convicts them, the impact on Americans engaged in protected First Amendment activities will be immediate and profound, given the pace, scope and nature of secret-making within the federal government today. As a defense motion to dismiss [the case] asserts: "The government's construction of [the Espionage Act] would allow for the punishment of any private citizen who obtains classified information—regardless of how or why—and then discloses it to another private citizen."

Even some Justice Department officials concede that prosecution of a journalist under the Espionage Act would raise "legitimate and serious issues." Yet they press on.

If the approach that federal prosecutors and, thus far, one federal judge embrace is allowed to stand, Americans will move a long step toward a society in which citizens are permitted to receive only that information which the government authorizes or concocts. That may be a rational reading of the law, but it certainly would be a woeful misapprehension of First Amendment principles and the traditions that hold a democracy together.

We live in a time of fear, of course: fear of terrorism, fear of failure, fear that the malodorous whiff of desperation or abuse will saturate the political air. It drives our leaders' obsession with secrecy and our citizenry's acceptance of it.

It becomes the job of journalists therefore, to remind us from time to time that secrecy and security are not always the same thing.

Journalists Have a Duty to Fight Government Secrecy

Pete Weitzel

Pete Weitzel is the freedom of information coordinator for the Coalition of Journalists for Open Government, one of the founders of Florida's First Amendment Foundation, and a former president of the National Freedom of Information Coalition.

Government secrecy is a big and expensive business—and it's getting bigger and more costly. [In 2003], the federal government spent more than $6.5 billion classifying and de-classifying federal records. It marked 14.2 million documents as "Top Secret," "Secret" or "Classified," putting them under lock and key for a minimum of two years. The rate of classifi-cation—up 26 percent in 2003 and more than 40 percent since 9/11—is almost double that during the last several years of the Clinton presidency.

Increasing Government Secrecy

By one estimate, during the past 25 years the U.S. government has classified between 7.5 and 8 billion pages of informa-tion—enough to replace all 18 million books in the Library of Congress with shelf space to spare. This revelation prompted the Intelligence Security Oversight Office to suggest the secret keeping is excessive and [to] call for restraint. It warns the federal government is classifying so much that it is putting the very secrecy it prizes at risk. Even some members of Congress said "whoa" when the Central Intelligence Agency (CIA) cen-sors blacked more than half of the 500-page Senate report on pre-Iraq war intelligence. Four senators, including former Ma-jority Leader Trent Lott, filed a bill to create an independent panel to review similar classification decisions. Lott called the CIA's censorship "absolutely an insult."

Pete Weitzel, "The Steady March of Government Secrecy," *Neiman Reports*, fall 2004. Reproduced by permission.

There's no estimate of the number of documents exempted entirely or in part from discretionary disclosure under the Freedom of Information Act (FOIA). This act became law in 1967 and provided the first statutory right of access to federal government records. In 2003, there were 3.2 million requests for federal government records, a 36 percent increase in one year. About half of these were granted. The information "grants" frequently come with heavy and inconsistent redaction and only after long delay. (Indeed, the government's use of the term "grant" might be a warning; it suggests officials regard release of information to be a gift or favor rather than something that citizens have a right to.) [In 2003], it took the attorney general's office an average of 361 days to handle a "complex" request and 80 days to handle one given expedited processing.

The always-slow FOIA process became even more difficult shortly after John Ashcroft settled in as attorney general [in 2001]. He sent federal agencies a new directive on FOIA that reversed the policy of his predecessor, Janet Reno, who was the daughter of journalists. In 1993, Reno advised government departments to be proactive on behalf of the public in handling FOIA requests. Treat government information as inherently public, she advised, and do not invoke discretionary exemptions unless there is evidence of "foreseeable harm" as a result of making information public.

Conversely, Ashcroft advised that the federal government should be at least as committed to protecting national security, the effectiveness of law enforcement agencies, sensitive business information, and personal privacy. Under Ashcroft's directive, these interests are to be given "full and deliberate consideration" when an FOIA request is made. He told federal agencies to look for a "sound legal basis" to withhold information and let them know they'd find support in this approach from his department. Perhaps it's coincidental, but FOIA requests to the Justice Department fell by 70 percent the following year. It may also be coincidental that the classification of documents by [the] [J]ustice [Department]—which makes them exempt from FOIA—increased by 80 percent in 2003.

The Spread of Informal Secrecy

The examination of classification and FOIA records provides only a partial picture of government secrecy. There is nothing to hint at how many records are now off the books and hidden behind new or newly defined designations that comprise an informal but very real fourth level of classification. The culture of closure that dug its roots in the nation's capital after 9/11 is being imposed across the nation through federal funding mandates and nondisclosure agreements. By one estimate, as many as four million local and state officials could be effectively gagged by requiring them to sign don't show, don't tell agreements. Secrecy is trickling down to many state and local lawmakers as well as with efforts to close records and meetings. And audits conducted by news organizations in several states [in 2004] showed that only half of state and local officials complied with existing open records laws.

Much of this new federal secrecy was authorized by Congress in an orgy of "national security" legislation after the attacks on the World Trade Center and the Pentagon. Only now are many of the details of this secrecy legislation being discovered as federal agencies, most prominently the Department of Homeland Security [DHS], draft new rules to implement those laws and in doing so reveal some of the regulatory details.

Perhaps most troubling to emerge is a new Transportation Security Administration (TSA) regulation that gives muscle and reach to a three-decades-old term: Sensitive Security Information (SSI). The evolution is instructive. It shows how a shroud of secrecy can be subtly laid over government.

SSI dates to 1974 and a wave of airline hijackings, when Congress gave the Federal Aviation Administration (FAA) authority to gather information on people who booked airline passage. Congress said the FAA could withhold this and other SSI it gathered, if its release would be "detrimental to safety of airline passengers." By [the] summer [of 2004], SSI had morphed into something far different—and for open government advocates and working reporters, something far more ominous.

The shroud of secrecy that covers Washington today is so frightening . . . because it's become so routine. Secrecy is the standard, not the exception.

SSI now includes not just information on passenger screening and policing but also information related to infrastructure, which could, of course, apply to records about environmental threats. It might also apply to operations information. The language seems to also empower TSA and the Department of Transportation to extend security oversight—and its ability to seal sensitive information, however loosely defined—to local transit systems and to the transport of hazardous wastes on the nation's highways, and also to pipelines.

Translated into an "Interim Final Rule," legislative changes provide the new and larger Transportation Security Administration (TSA) and related departments with the authority to designate as SSI any information—whether they create it or collect it—about any form of transportation they regard as being in any way related to security. This includes state, regional and local records as well as federal documents. Certain agencies are empowered to execute nondisclosure agreements with state and local officials and private contractors to make sure they don't disclose the information. These nondisclosure agreements are a relatively new tool in the secrecy game, and they work because any breach carries a stiff fine and possible prison time.

The TSA regulations did not make news in Washington. Nor was much attention paid to an earlier set of regulations allowing the Department of Homeland Security to gather and seal vast amounts of information on the nation's infrastructure or a recent directive on instructing DHS employees to mark sensitive but unclassified information as being for official use only.

Indeed, one reason the shroud of secrecy that covers Washington today is so frightening is because it's become so routine. Secrecy is the standard, not the exception. Any presumption of transparency has been lost.

Failing to Get Information

The Freedom of Information Act was passed by Congress as an amendment to the 1946 Administrative Procedure Act (APA). This earlier act had required federal agencies to keep the public informed about rules and procedures and said members of the public should be able to participate in the rulemaking process. At the same time, APA suggested there were exceptions to openness: Information might be withheld on "any function . . . requiring secrecy in the public interest."

FOIA became law after a 16-year campaign by journalism organizations and others to promote the citizen's "right to know." It was strengthened in 1974 and expanded to include electronic records in 1995. But FOIA was never an easy process. Procedural delays are built in; for example, an agency doesn't even have to respond for 20 days. And there is a cumbersome review process: Information can be withheld if it falls within any one of nine broad categories of exemption.

Under the [George W.] Bush administration, there has been progressive closure with the spread and speed of secrecy increasing after 9/11 through legislation, presidential orders, department directives, and broad administrative legal interpretations. The Ashcroft memo set the tone, rewriting the rules of engagement to give bureaucrats who wish to play hardball the encouragement to do so.

Some examples of how the secrecy game is now being played:

- The Justice Department [in 2004] turned down an FOIA request for a list of terrorism-related indictments, then rejected a follow-up request for copies of all of the press releases issued on those individual indictments. The reason: invasion of privacy.

- Justice also turned down a request for information on registered foreign government lobbyists. The reason: The database is so old, the department said, that if we try to run it the system will crash.

- The Labor Department's Mind Health and Safety Administration refused a reporter's request for biographical information on a new deputy secretary. The reason: privacy.

- TSA turned down a request for information about its "no fly" list of those automatically pulled from airport security lines for a more thorough screening. It cited both privacy and SSI as reasons for their withholding documents. A federal judge in a suit brought by the American Civil Liberties Union (ACLU) ruled that the names withheld had appeared in newspaper articles and other information was "innocuous" and in some instances had been used in public slide presentations. The judge ordered the information to be released.

- The TSA refused the request of a Minneapolis reporter who thought it would be a public service to let people know what items commonly carried by airline passengers frequently set off airport screening machines. The reason: SSI.

- After White House Chief of Staff Andrew Card sent a memo ordering a review of Web postings in 2002, at least 6,000 documents were being pulled from government Web sites. There was no way of knowing the nature or extent of information withheld from government Web sites since then, but one recent incident hints at the new creativity of closure. The Center for Army Lessons Learned posted a book-length critique of Operation Iraqi Freedom with this disclaimer. "This document has security functions enabled to prevent printing, downloading, cutting and pasting."

- The Environmental Protection Agency took another approach: eliminate the evidence. Its annual Toxics Release inventory, typically a 400-page report containing data and analysis of the nation's chemical plants and potential dangers, was reduced to six summary pages [in 2004] as a result of industry lobbying. That left environmental writers who regularly use the inventory in computer-assisted reporting without a byte to chew on.

- The Pentagon classified the army's report on abuses at Abu Ghraib prison [in Iraq] as "secret" and kept the marking even after photos taken by service personnel became public. The Information Security Oversight Office (ISOO) challenged both the legality and the wisdom of the Pentagon's action. ISOO Director William Leonard noted that information that reveals violations of the law cannot be classified. He questioned the "bureaucratic impulse" to mark as "secret" one passage discussing the potential political fallout of releasing the report. "It's difficult to see how that information [could] . . . damage national security," Leonard observed.

Frequently . . . Leonard has said that over-classification hurts the entire system by making secrets less secure because it inevitably invites leakage from "the highest levels of our government." Within a month of Leonard sending this memo to the Pentagon, *U.S. News & World Report* reported that it had obtained all 106 classified annexes to the army's Abu Ghraib report.

The Patriot Act, which became law just six weeks after the [September 2001] terrorist attacks, expands the FBI's investigatory powers. Among these powers is the ability to obtain secret court orders to seize personal and private business records and to eavesdrop on telephone and e-mail conversations. It permits secret court hearings of alleged terrorists. Little is known—not even the names—of more than 1,200 presumably terrorist-related arrests and the deportation of at least 750 people. Nor does anyone outside the government know how many court docket entries have been erased or simply not entered. Secret federal court hearings have been held with no public record of when or where or who is being tried. Everyone involved is gagged. The Supreme Court even allowed the Justice Department to file a sealed brief in one case. Such is the level of paranoia about secrecy in the government that when the ACLU filed a suit challenging Patriot Act provisions, it was prohibited from going public with the details of the suit. Its press release announcing the in-court protest was censored.

The war on terrorism seems to have put a damper on aggressive reporting and watchdog writing about efforts by government to 'safeguard information.'

The Reporters Committee for Freedom of the Press is trying to track down information on reports of at least 50 secret federal court cases across the country. Does this attempt to get information encourage similar closure in other courts? In July [2004], public defenders in Washington, D.C., filed a petition listing 200 superior court cases that had been closed and records sealed.

[In 2004], the Congressional Research Service observed that one consequence of the Homeland Security Act—creating a huge new government department to oversee the nation's internal protection from terrorism—is that vast amounts of data are now being marked "sensitive" as they are being created or gathered, and thus they are "born protected." Yet no criteria have been established for this marking, nor is there any provision for review of the decision to "safeguard" this information from public view.

Journalists' Responses to Secrecy

News reporting on all of this has been limited and tepid. Instead, the ground wars in Afghanistan and then Iraq, the broader war on terrorism, and inside-the-Beltway [federal government] obsession with partisan politics dominate the news. The war on terrorism seems to have put a damper on aggressive reporting and watchdog writing about efforts by government to "safeguard information."

There have been a few high-profile exceptions. Vice President Dick Cheney's refusal to make public information on his energy task force has been widely reported, as has the ban on photographing of coffins of military personnel and the stamping of "Top Secret" on the already public photos of prisoner abuse at Abu Ghraib. Lawsuits challenging secret court proceedings have also been widely reported.

A reporter from the (Mami) *Daily Business Review*, Dan Christensen, had begun a year-long reporting assignment on secret hearings being held in federal courts, when he saw an unusual entry on a docket sheet, asked a few questions, and got stonewalled. Later, the U.S. Supreme Court sanctioned the approach of secret dockets and hearings, even to the point of allowing the Solicitor General to file a sealed brief. And few newspapers carried the first day story from The Associated Press (AP) when U.S. marshals seized and destroyed reporters' tape recordings of a speech given by [Supreme Court] Justice

Antonin Scalia. The *Washington Post* did not mention it. The *New York Times* carried a single paragraph.

Paradoxically, many of the nation's journalism-related foundations and organizations have taken notice of this issue. [From 2000 to 2004], the John S. and James L. Knight Foundation and the McCormick Tribune Foundation have given grants of more than $7.6 million for freedom of information projects in the United States. One of those projects is the Coalition of Journalists for Open Government, which began with Knight support [in] January [2004]. Its mission is to coordinate the freedom of information efforts of its member organizations, now numbering 27. I was hired as its coordinator. Members of the coalition include the American Society of Newspaper Editors (ASNE), Radio-Television News Directors Association (RTNDA), Society of Professional Journalists (SPJ), the Newspaper Association of America (NAA), and Reporters Committee for Freedom of the Press.

In April [2004], the President of the AP, Tom Curley, called for a new assault on government secrecy. It was time, Curley said, for journalists to "push back" at all levels against government efforts to close records and meetings. The AP, he pledged, would start more aggressively reporting on open government issues and would support FOIA audits in every state. Since then, there has been a marked increase in AP reports on secrecy and closure. Curley also said AP would help to establish a governmental affairs office in Washington, D.C., to monitor and lobby on these issues. No details of that initiative have been announced, but AP officials are meeting with representatives of journalism organizations, FOIA attorneys, and open government advocates as part of their planning.

ASNE, SPJ and RTNDA have legal counsel in Washington, but their employment is part-time and some of the lawyers' time must be devoted to nonlegislative matters. The most consistent and concerted lobbying by media organizations is done by the National Association of Broadcasters and the

NAA, the respective ownership organizations for television and newspapers. However, their focus is on business issues. NAA does some lobbying on FOIA issues and recently was able to get the House to nudge [the Department of] Health and Human Services for a much-needed clarification of its regulations implementing the Health Insurance Portability and Accountability Act (HIPAA). Those regulations effectively close off reporter access to critical information on victims of crime, accidents and disasters.

There has been no coordinated information gathering or strategic planning about secrecy and reporters' access to information within the journalism community or among its organizations. No one looks at upcoming federal legislation or monitors departmental policies and regulations to identify such access issues. While the individual organizations sometimes send letters of protest or submit comments urging changes in regulations, no concerted legislative strategy or proactive plan is in place to attempt to reverse the pattern of increasing closure. Media organizations tend to go their separate ways. When they do come together, it has usually been out of common frustration and to fight for a common cause, such as freedom of information.

The federal government ... demands that we, as a people, sacrifice other freedoms to achieve freedom from fear.

Historical Parallels

What is starting to happen today has a parallel a half century ago. In the late 1940's, Basil L. Walters, executive editor of the *Chicago Daily News* and chair of ASNE's World Freedom of Information Committee, said that in their own communities U.S. newspapers were "permitting the people's right to information to go by default." The first step he proposed: Drop the word "World" from the committee name and focus on problems in their hometowns.

At this time, there were few if any legal experts on government access, and editors across the country were increasingly frustrated and unsure how to respond when local government officials closed meetings or denied access to records. ASNE hired attorney and legal scholar Harold L. Cross to analyze the laws across the country and make recommendations. His book, *The People's Right to Know*, set the stage for a national campaign by ASNE and other journalism organizations that would continue into the 1960's.

The predecessor to the Society of Professional Journalists, Sigma Delta Chi (SDX), developed a model open meetings law and pushed for its adoption. At the time, only one state had such a law. The campaign slowly built support, and change came, a piece at a time. For example, the first open meeting bill in Florida was introduced in 1953 by a delegation from the St. Petersburg area that had been lobbied by their local SDX chapter. The bill won initial support in the house but never budged in the senate. Similar bills were introduced in every session from 1957 to 1965 and met the same fate. In 1967, using a model law clipped from the SDX magazine, *Quill*, a senator from Gainesville, with the support of a reapportioned, reform-minded legislature, managed to get Florida's much-admired "Government in the Sunshine" law passed. The political culture and climate for openness also evolved in many other states during those years. By 1967, at least 35 had adopted some form of open government legislation, and the federal government had approved the Freedom of Information Act.

It's worth considering another historic parallel. When victory in World War II was in sight, if still a long way off, President Franklin D. Roosevelt challenged the nation in his 11th State of the Union address to think beyond the war to issues of "economic security, social security, and moral security." Only when we establish each of these, he said, will we have gained true national security. Today the federal government treats security as having only one dimension and demands that we, as a people, sacrifice other freedoms to achieve freedom from fear. If we as journalists allow this to happen, we will not only have forsaken our mission but our country. The strength of our nation is protection of its many freedoms—the first of which must be the freedom to have access to information about the decisions our government leaders make. Without that, all other freedoms are less secure.

Organizations to Contact

The editors have compiled the following list of organizations concerned with the issues debated in this book. The descriptions are derived from materials provided by the organizations. All have publications or information available for interested readers. The list was compiled on the date of publication of the present volume; the information provided here may change. Be aware that many organizations take several weeks or longer to respond to inquiries, so allow as much time as possible.

American Civil Liberties Union (ACLU)
125 Broad St., 18th Floor., New York, NY   10004
(212) 549-2500 • fax: (212) 549-2646
e-mail: aclu@aclu.org
Web site: www.aclu.org

The ACLU is a national organization that defends Americans' civil rights as guaranteed in the U.S. Constitution. It advocates freedom of all forms of speech, including pornography, flag-burning, and political protest. The ACLU offers numerous reports, fact sheets, and policy statements on free speech issues, which are freely available on its Web site. Some of these publications include "Free Speech Under Fire," "Freedom of Expression," and, for students, "Ask Sybil Liberty About Your Right to Free Expression."

American Library Association (ALA)
50 E. Huron St., Chicago, IL   60611
(800) 545-2433 • fax: (312) 440-9374
e-mail: ala@ala.org
Web site: www.ala.org

The ALA is the United States' primary professional organization for librarians. Through its Office for Intellectual Freedom (OIF), the ALA supports free access to libraries and library materials. The OIF also monitors and opposes efforts to ban books from libraries. Its publications, which are freely available on its Web site, include "Intellectual Freedom and Censorship Q & A," the "Library Bill of Rights," and the "Freedom to Read Statement."

Concerned Women for America (CWA)
1015 Fifteenth St. NW, Suite 1100, Washington, DC   20005
(202) 488-7000 • fax: (202) 488-0806
Web site: www.cwfa.org

CWA is a membership organization that promotes Christian values and works to create a society that is conducive to forming families and raising healthy children. Opposition to pornography is one of CWA's six major focuses. Its publications include the monthly *Family Voice* magazine, which has addressed such topics as Internet filters in libraries.

Electronic Frontier Foundation (EFF)
454 Shotwell St., San Francisco, CA   94110-1914
(415) 436-9333 • fax (415) 436-9993
e-mail: information@eff.org
Web site: www.eff.org

EFF is a nonprofit, nonpartisan organization that works to protect privacy, freedom of speech and other rights in the digital world. Fighting censorship on the Internet is one of its core missions. Its publications, which are freely available on its Web site, include a "Legal Guide for Bloggers" and white papers such as "Noncommercial Email Lists: Collateral Damage in the Fight Against Spam."

Family Research Council (FRC)
801 G St. NW, Washington, DC   20001
(202) 393-2100 • fax: (202) 393-2134
Web site: www.frc.org

The FRC is a faith-based organization that seeks to promote marriage and family. It believes that pornography harms women, children and families, and therefore the FRC seeks to strengthen current obscenity laws. It publishes a variety of books, policy papers, fact sheets, and other materials, including the brochure "Dealing with Pornography: A Practical Guide for Protecting Your Family and Your Community" and the book *Protecting Your Child in an X-Rated World: What You Need to Know to Make a Difference.*

Federal Communications Commission (FCC)
445 Twelfth St. SW, Washington, DC   20554
(888) 225-5322 • fax: (866) 418-0232
e-mail: fccinfo@fcc.gov
Web site: www.fcc.gov

The FCC is an independent government agency responsible for regulating telecommunications. Among other duties, it enforces federal laws related to broadcast indecency. The FCC publishes various reports, updates, and reviews that can be accessed online at its Web site.

Foundation for Individual Rights in Education (FIRE)
601 Walnut St., Suite 510, Philadelphia, PA   19106
(215) 717-3473 • fax: (215) 717-3440
e-mail: fire@thefire.org
Web site: www.thefire.org

FIRE was founded in 1999 to defend the rights of students and professors at American colleges and universities. The group provides legal assistance to students and professors who feel that their individual rights, particularly their rights to free speech, have been violated. Its publications include *FIRE's Guide to Free Speech on Campus* and "Spotlight: The Campus Freedom Resource," which contains information about speech codes at specific colleges and universities.

Freedom Forum
1101 Wilson Blvd., Arlington, VA   22209
(703) 528-0800 • fax: (703) 284-3770
e-mail: news@freedomforum.org
Web site: www.freedomforum.org

The Freedom Forum was founded in 1991 to defend a free press and free speech. It operates the Newseum (a museum of news and the news media) and the First Amendment Center, which works to educate the public about free speech and other First Amendment issues. Its publications include an annual "State of the First Amendment" survey, and the First Amendment Center maintains on its Web site a "First Amendment Library" that serves as a clearinghouse for judicial, legislative, and other material on First Amendment freedoms.

Free Expression Policy Project (FEPP)
161 Avenue of the Americas, 12th Floor.
New York, NY   10013
(212) 998-6733 • fax: (212) 995-4550
Web site: www.fepproject.org

FEPP is a project of the Democracy Program at New York University School of Law's Brennan Center for Justice. FEPP promotes freedom of expression, but in a "non-absolutist" fashion; it believes that certain forms of speech, such as harassing and threatening speech, are not entitled to First Amendment protection. Its publications include fact sheets, commentaries, and policy reports, which are freely available on its Web site.

Free Speech Coalition
PO Box 10480, Canoga Park, CA   91309
(818) 348-9373 • fax: (818) 886-5914
Web site: www.freespeechcoalition.com

The coalition is a trade association that represents members of the adult entertainment industry. It seeks to protect the industry from attempts to censor pornography. Its publications include the journal *Free Speaker* and the weekly *Free Speech X-Press*.

Morality in Media (MIM)
475 Riverside Dr., Suite 239, New York, NY   10115
(212) 870-3222 • fax: (212) 870-2765

e-mail: mim@moralityinmedia.org
Web site: www.moralityinmedia.org

MIM is a national interfaith organization that fights obscenity and indecency in the media. It works to educate the public on obscenity issues and maintains the National Obscenity Law Center, a clearinghouse of legal materials on obscenity law. Its publications include the reports "Stranger in the House," "Pornography's Effects on Adults and Children," and the bi-monthly *Morality in Media Newsletter*.

National Coalition Against Censorship (NCAC)
275 Seventh Ave., New York, NY 10001
(212) 807-6222 • fax: (212) 807-6245
e-mail: ncac@ncac.org
Web site: www.ncac.org

NCAC is an alliance of national not-for-profit organizations, including literary, artistic, religious, educational, professional, labor, and civil liberties groups. The coalition works to defend freedom of thought, inquiry, and expression and to fight censorship. Its Web site provides access to press releases, legal briefs, and congressional testimony on censorship issues.

National Coalition for the Protection of Children and Families
800 Compton Rd., Suite 9224, Cincinnati, OH 45231
(513) 521-6227 • fax: (513) 521-6337
e-mail: ncpcf@nationalcoalition.org
Web site: www.nationalcoalition.org

The coalition is a Christian organization that encourages traditional sexual ethics and fights pornography. It encourages strong regulation of adult bookstores and the use of Internet filters in public libraries. Its publications include the *Library Protection Plan* and the booklet *Pornography: The Deconstruction of Human Sexuality*.

Rutherford Institute
PO Box 7482, Charlottesville, VA 22906-7482
(434) 978-3888 • fax: (434) 978-1789
e-mail: staff@rutherford.org
Web site: www.rutherford.org

The Rutherford Institute is a conservative organization that was founded to defend First Amendment rights, including the right to freedom of speech and freedom of religion. The institute provides free legal aid to people who believe that their rights to these freedoms have been violated. The Rutherford Institute's publications, which are freely available on its Web site, include "Zero Tolerance for God? Religious Expression in the Workplace" and "Through the Looking Glass: What Are Young People Learning from Unconstitutional Religious Censorship?"

Bibliography

Books

Jerome A. Barron and C. Thomas Dienes

First Amendment Law in a Nutshell. St. Paul, MN: Thomson/West, 2004.

David B. Cohen and John W. Wells, eds.

American National Security and Civil Liberties in an Era of Terrorism. New York: Palgrave Macmillan, 2004.

Raphael Cohen-Almagor

The Scope of Tolerance: Studies on the Costs of Free Expression and Freedom of the Press. New York: Routledge, 2005.

Anthony Cortese

Opposing Hate Speech. Westport, CT: Praeger, 2006.

Richard Delgado and Jean Stefancic

Understanding Words That Wound. Boulder, CO: Westview Press, 2004.

Donald Alexander Downs

Restoring Free Speech and Liberty on Campus. Oakland, CA: Independent Institute, 2005.

Mike Godwin

Cyber Rights: Defending Free Speech in the Digital Age. Cambridge, MA: MIT Press, 2003.

Jon B. Gould

Speak No Evil: The Triumph of Hate Speech Regulation. Chicago: University of Chicago Press, 2005.

Marjorie Heins, Christina Cho, and Ariel Feldman	*Internet Filters: A Public Policy Report*. New York: Brennan Center for Justice, 2006.
Gil Reavill	*Smut: A Sex Industry Insider (and Concerned Father) Says Enough Is Enough*. New York: Sentinel, 2005.
Charles H. Sides	*Freedom of Information in a Post 9-11 World*. Amityville, NY: Baywood, 2006.
Harvey A. Silvergate, David French, and Greg Lukianoff	*FIRE's Guide to Free Speech on Campus*. Philadelphia: Foundation for Individual Rights in Education, 2005.
Joseph Vogel	*Free Speech 101: The Utah Valley Uproar over Michael Moore*. Silverson, ID: WindRiver, 2006.
Amy E. White	*Virtually Obscene: The Case for an Uncensored Internet*. Jefferson, NC: McFarland, 2006.
John Ziegler	*The Death of Free Speech: How Our Broken National Dialogue Has Killed the Truth and Divided America*. Nashville,TN: Cumberland House, 2005.

Periodicals

Rizwan Ahmed	"Battling the Censor," *New Statesman*, August 28, 2006.
David Aikman	"Train Wreck Coming," *Christianity Today*, October 2006.

Gerard Alexander   "Illiberal Europe," *Weekly Standard*, April 10, 2006.

Jonathan Alter   "A Shabby Fiesta of Hypocrisy," *Newsweek*, November 29, 2004.

Eric Alterman   "Fool Me Once . . . ," *Nation*, January 23, 2006.

Sara-Ellen Amster   "Teaching Students to Be Citizens," *San Diego Union Tribune*, April 13, 2006.

Kurt Andersen   "What the [bleep]?!," *New York*, June 5, 2006.

Yudhijit Bhattacharjee   "Scientific Openness: Should Academics Self-Censor Their Findings on Terrorism?," *Science*, May 19, 2006.

David Blunkett   "Religious Hatred Is No Laughing Matter," *Observer* (UK), December 12, 2004.

Gary Bouma   "Why Costello Is Wrong on Vilification Laws," *Age*, June 1, 2004.

William F. Buckley Jr.   "The Search for Decency," *National Review*, May 22, 2006.

Tim Cavanaugh   "Cartoons Make Cowards of Us All," *Reason*, May 2006.

Christian Science Monitor   "From China to Denmark, Media Lessons," February 7, 2006.

Ronald K. L. Collins and David L. Hudson Jr.	"Laws Against Funeral Protests Strike at the First Amendment," *Legal Intelligencer*, April 21, 2006.
David Coursey	"I, Censor?," *eWeek*, September 8, 2005.
Charles Davis	"More Daunting Tests Ahead Pitting 'Right to Know' Against 'Need to Know,'" *IRE Journal*, January–February 2004.
Simon Dumenco	"The FCC Thinks You Would Look Totally Hot in a Diaper," *Advertising Age*, June 5, 2006.
Bruce Einhorn	"Search Engines Censured for Censorship," *Business Week Online*, August 10, 2006. www.businessweek.com
Daveed Garnstein-Ross	"Legislating Religious Correctness," *Weekly Standard*, October 27, 2005.
Economist	"An Indecent Proposal," July 23, 2005.
Elizabeth Guider	"Showbiz in Shackles," *Variety*, March 13, 2006.
E. Herman	"A Post-September 11 Balancing Act," *Journal of Government Information*, vol. 30, no. 1, 2004.
Mike Hudson and Chad Graham	"The Big Chill Censorship," *Advocate*, May 11, 2004.

Seth Killian   "Violent Video Game Players Myste-
                        riously Avoid Killing Selves, Others,"
                        NCAC Censorship News, Winter
                        2003–2004.

Faisal Kutty   "Danish Cartoons," *Catholic New
                        Times*, March 19, 2006.

J. F. O. Mcallister   "Drawing a Fine Line," *Time Interna-
                        tional* (Europe Edition), February 20,
                        2006. www.time.com/time/europe/.

Helen Nguyen   "2nd Circuit Rules School Violated
                        Student's Rights in President Bush
                        Shirt Censorship Incident," *Long Is-
                        land (NY) Business News*, September
                        15, 2006.

Valeriu Nicolae   "Words That Kill," *Index on Censor-
                        ship*, January 2006.

John Pilger   "The Real First Casualty of War,"
                        New Statesman, April 24, 2006.

Matthew Quirk   "The Web Police," *Atlantic Monthly*,
                        May 2006.

J. Max Robins   "Playing Dirty," *Broadcasting &
                        Cable*, March 27, 2006.

Richard   "Regulation, Responsibility and the
Sambrook   Case Against Censorship," *Index on
                        Censorship*, January 2006.

Ziauddin Sardar   "Freedom of Speech Is Islamic, Too,"
                        New Statesman, February 13, 2006.

Gabriel
Schoenfeld

"Has the *New York Times* Violated the Espionage Act?," *Commentary*, March 2006.

Bruce Shapiro

"More Leaks, Please!" *Nation*, December 5, 2005.

Tom Teodorczuk

"Classified Material," *New Statesman*, August 14, 2006.

USA Today

"Amendment Supporters Exaggerate Threat to Flag," (editorial) June 14, 2005.

David Wallis

"The Wrong Lesson," *Reason*, August–September 2004.

Wall Street Journal

"Fit and Unfit to Print," June 30, 2006.

Thomas E.
Wheeler II

"Lessons from *The Lord of the Flies*," *Journal of Internet Law*, July 2006.

Jay Woodruff

"See No Evil?" *Entertainment Weekly*, August 6, 2004.

Index